do you need a financial adviser?

MARK NIND

MEMOIRS

Cirencester

Published by Memoirs

MEMOIRS
PUBLISHING

25 Market Place, Cirencester, Gloucestershire, GL7 2NX
info@memoirsbooks.co.uk www.memoirspublishing.com

Copyright ©Mark Nind, November 2012

First published in England, November 2012

Book jacket design Ray Lipscombe

ISBN 978-1-909304-62-8

Printed in England

do you need a financial adviser?

CONTENTS

INTRODUCTION

INTRODUCTION

Background

I am an independent financial adviser and have been since 1996. Before that I worked for a major high street bank. You could therefore say that I have worked in financial services for most of my working life.

I would like to be in a position to say that financial advisers have always had a great reputation and have provided a great service to all. In some cases, this has been true but that hasn't always happened.

Since leaving the bank, I have worked for eight different firms which offer financial advice and have seen and heard different ways of advising clients. Much earlier in my career, financial advisers were more akin to sales people than to professional advisers. Generally speaking, there was very little in the way of advice and not much by the way of servicing or ensuring that the client remained on track with their plans. The trend has moved away from sales. Nowadays, it is the emphasis on advice and on-going servicing that plays an ever-important part.

When I first started work as a financial adviser, no qualifications were required. Virtually anyone could be a financial adviser! Many in the industry recall of times when the only tool you needed to get started was a telephone directory. The emphasis was not on 'what you knew' but rather 'who you knew'.

In the early days, many advisers were self employed and relied on commission as their only way of earning a living. New starters were encouraged to sell to their friends and family. Once this source of new 'customers' had been exhausted, there was often little prospect of them earning a decent living. For many, it was a brief and painful introduction to financial services. Thankfully, those days are behind us.

It was towards the latter part of the 1990s when it became compulsory for those advising to be qualified. The Chartered Insurance

Institute's Financial Planning Certificate became the base qualification required.

The emphasis to further improve standards continues. Advisers are encouraged to become even more qualified than they used to be. In addition, there is annual testing to ensure skills and knowledge are kept up to date. The Chartered Financial Planner accolade has also been introduced.

The Financial Services Authority (FSA) launched the Retail Distribution Review (RDR) in 2006. One of the outcomes of this review has resulted in the bar being raised even higher. As from December 2012, the Financial Planning Certificate is no longer sufficient. Qualifications and Credit Framework (QCF) Level 4 / The Diploma in Financial Planning will soon be the required benchmark needed before advice can be given.

Some advisers will choose to leave the profession rather than attain the extra qualifications that will soon be needed. Arguably, those that remain will be more professional than when I started out many years ago.

It is worth mentioning, at this stage, that the Chartered Insurance Institute (CII) is just one of several accreditation bodies approved by the Financial Services Authority (FSA).

IS ADVICE NEEDED?

There is no doubt that most financial advisers offer a valuable service to their clients. With others, it is difficult to see what value is added.

Professional standards have improved over the period of time that I have been involved with financial services. Whether all clients have benefited from the advice they have received is difficult to analyse. I am, however, aware that there have been cases where it is obvious that members of the public have made big mistakes as a result of not seeking advice. Again, I am aware of many instances where such mistakes have been extremely costly.

This book is about looking at many areas where advice is traditionally offered. Its main aim is to provide information for you to consider whether you should "do it yourself" or seek professional advice. There are a number of places you can go for advice. This may be the traditional "face to face" way. Alternatively, you could look towards other sources. The internet, for example, offers a wide range of different sources that can be extremely useful.

The aim of this book is to let you judge whether advice is really required in any given circumstance. It may result in you seeking advice whereas before you may not have thought this necessary. Alternatively, you may end up re-appraising what you get from your adviser and decide whether you should continue with them or look at alternatives.

There is a vast catalogue of information available on the internet. Where to look on the website is the part that can be particularly time consuming. After all, it is difficult to look for something when you do not know precisely what you are looking for. Whether you have the time to look for the information that you need or are prepared to pay for an adviser to do the work is the question only you can answer. Opinions will differ.

REASONS TO USE AN ADVISER

The main reasons can be summarised as follows:

Save time

You may not have the time or inclination to understand the various financial plans available. Whilst you may have a good idea of what you want, you may be happy to pay for someone to do the research rather than do it yourself.

For instance, I may be able to learn plumbing. Rather than go through the process, it may be just as easy to pay a professional and let me get on with what I am already trained and qualified to do.

Prevent mistakes being made

Left to your own devices, there is the possibility that you may make mistakes in the decisions you take. Some mistakes you may ultimately become aware of. In other instances, you may never become aware of any errors that are made.

You may invest in funds that are totally inappropriate. For example, someone I knew invested a significant sum of money in a FTSE 100 tracker fund. This was after seeing an advert in a newspaper. The value of the investment fell. Even though this should have been viewed as a medium to long term investment, this fall in value was not palatable with that particular person. They immediately withdrew the funds and suffered the loss. They relied too much on the brand of the firm offering the plan without appearing to realise what it was they were actually investing in.

There are many examples of where you may never know that you have made a mistake. One area could be to do with not fully being aware of the options available. For instance, a smoker may be able to obtain a higher pension (annuity rate) than a non-smoker. If they are unaware that smoker rates are available, they may unwittingly receive a lower pension than they could have otherwise obtained. To emphasise this point further, you do not have to draw your pension from the insurance company you have been saving with. Other insurance companies may be able to offer better terms for your particular circumstances. This is what is referred to as an 'Open Market Option'.

There are other circumstances where you may not be aware of what is available to you due to the changing nature of financial advice.

Clients don't know what they don't know

There are always new innovations and consequently more products being introduced. The best solution for you may be a plan or product that you are totally unaware of. A good adviser should keep up to date with changes in legislation and be aware of new plans that are introduced.

A second opinion

You may have strong views on where and how your funds should be invested. Rather than rushing headlong and investing £100,000 in the "Peruvian lama" fund, you may feel the need to just check and ensure that you are not making a grave mistake.

Perhaps a more realistic example would be in respect of some of the property schemes that have been 'promoted'. Some of the offerings I have seen for overseas holiday properties look more like holiday brochures than what you would normally expect to see where investments are promoted. Care should be exercised. If you are tempted to invest, a second opinion should be considered appropriate in these and many other instances.

To help with the vast choice of financial products

There is an ever increasing choice of products available. It is difficult for an individual to keep fully up to date with everything that is going on. Legislation constantly changes and this has an impact on what new plans are introduced. A good financial adviser will discuss your priorities, assess your needs and make recommendations based on their knowledge and experience.

One size cannot fit all! You could be aged 20 or 60. You may have no dependants or you may have several. You may want to retire at age 55 or 75. You may be a non taxpayer or a higher rate taxpayer. You may wish to take a high risk attitude to investing or be ultra cautious. Usually, there are different solutions for different circumstances.

Imagine a scenario where it is rumoured that it is best to invest in China. This could be via media coverage, 'canteen gossip' or any number of different suggestions. For starters, this would be unsuitable for cautious investors. If you have an investment horizon of less than 5 years, I would also suggest that it was unsuitable. At the very least, you should be fully aware of the risks with this type of investment rather than just believe that you have access to information that few others are aware of.

I would suggest that guidance from an adviser to help in these situations would be needed and should be sought.

To educate and inform

A good adviser can help decipher current events. This may include proposed changes to the budget. The details of the budget can be quickly interpreted so that you become aware of how any changes to tax, trusts and pension legislation, for example, would impact on you.

Many advisers believe that their job is to educate their clients in financial matters. Rather than just facilitate transactions, they aim to improve the client's knowledge. This is likely to include the correcting of any misconceptions that may have arisen due to the press and television coverage of financial matters.

To help create a balanced portfolio

Investment is about managing expectations. This involves preparing for the potential falls in value as well as the expected increases. The first part of this process is assessing a client's attitude to risk (see Chapter 7). Generally speaking; the higher the risk, the higher the returns. This is likely to be especially true in the medium to long term.

Having ascertained risk, the basis of a portfolio can be constructed. Such a portfolio ought to reflect the attitude to risk that you are prepared to take with your investments. It would also be sufficiently diversified so that you were not exposed to any particular sector or asset class.

To help you save

A financial adviser will help you to think about your long-term future. They will also help you maintain the discipline required to save. The objective could be retirement planning, wedding expenses, education costs or, indeed, any medium to long term capital requirement. The aim is to put an achievable plan in place. Money is then put aside in order to achieve your goals.

To keep you on track

Once a plan has been put in place, it needs to be reviewed. Regular reviews are an important way of making sure you remain on track.

People's circumstances change. For example, a promotion could increase your income and thus increase your overall living standards. This could lead to you having more surplus funds available in order to improve your standard of living in retirement.

Changing market conditions mean that even the best plans will need to be updated. Other factors including divorce or an inheritance can also have significant implications. Your plan is likely to need amending to take account of these and other major events that impact on your financial wellbeing.

In short, nothing remains constant and a financial adviser can be invaluable for ensuring that your 'plan' is kept up to date and on target.

For peace of mind

Money can be a very emotive subject. It is a constant struggle to try and remove the emotion in making financial decisions. Stockmarket based investments can be volatile. It is easy for the inexperienced investor to make mistakes due to the fear of losing all their money when markets appear to be in freefall. Equally, an investor could invest in fads such as technology. This can be fuelled by media coverage or even a tip from a friend or colleague. Some information from the media can be exaggerated so much as to be viewed as misleading.

Taking advice before making any decisions takes the emphasis away from you and puts it in the hands of an adviser. Any advice given would be there to be scrutinised and would give comfort in knowing that a degree of care had been taken in arriving at the most appropriate solution for you.

REASONS NOT TO USE AN ADVISER

They can be expensive

There can be a number of layers involved in the advice process. There is the product provider which has traditionally been an insurance company. They may reach the public directly via advertisements through a number of different channels.

Most insurance companies now provide access to specialist external fund managers. This can be (but not always) at an extra charge which adds another layer of cost.

Then there are the costs for advice. Traditionally this was by way of commissions. These have to be paid from somewhere – typically from the investment or additional charges. Fund based renewal commission can also be a feature of an adviser's remuneration. This is typically an extra ½% to 1% per annum and is by way of an additional charge. I have seen where some advisers charge over and above this. Whether these charges are appropriate and justifiable can be debated.

More and more advisers are moving towards fees as an alternative to commission. In some cases, commissions are being re-branded as fees. To demonstrate this point, what is the difference between 1% per annum being paid by way of fund based renewal commission and 1% per annum being paid as an annual fee with this being paid out of the investment? The answer is - not much.

It can be debated whether charges or performance should be the dominant factor when choosing an investment. One main factor is that charges can be determined in advance. Investment performance cannot. Another point is that many decisions to invest in funds are based on past performance.

It can be particularly frustrating for a client to pay fees or commissions for an adviser's services only for the investment to under-perform. It cannot be too surprising for a client, in these circumstances, to wonder why they used an adviser as they would feel that they couldn't have done any worse themselves. That being said, I cannot envisage any situation where an adviser would deliberately set out to invest a client's funds badly.

I have noticed that when investments are doing well, not much attention is given to the charges by those investing. On the other hand, when investment returns are low, any charges stick out like a 'sore thumb' and erode the investment returns.

The objective should be for the investor to gain from the advice experience. The danger is that charges levied by the adviser could cancel out any benefit that may have been added.

They may not add value

Can an adviser do any better than you?

There are many that question the value an adviser can add. I would cite the company Hargreaves Lansdown as a successful formula that allows an investor to select their own funds. Access to a vast number of funds and providers are made available to let the client decide. Products such as an ISA or a pension are made available. These are at a competitive price. They then provide the facility for an investor to select from a number of different funds from most fund providers. Individual shares can also be selected. Care needs to be taken as advice is not given for their internet offerings. Mistakes can therefore be made and it is the investor that would need to take full responsibility for the choices they make.

They may not know any more than you do

Advisers are required to be more qualified than they were years ago. I would like to state that, generally speaking, a fully qualified adviser is likely to know a great deal more than the general public.

Advisers shouldn't be viewed as fortune tellers or predictors. They cannot gaze into a crystal ball and predict the future. Some clients expect financial advisers to do just that. If an adviser talks with any authority about how the FTSE 100 is likely to perform or what the financial climate will look like, I would suggest they are doing their clients an injustice.

We can all be wise after the event. Sense can be made of virtually anything. As they say, hindsight is a wonderful thing. Shares fell quite dramatically towards the end of 2008. Looking back, March 2009 would appear to be the low point. Since March 2009, shares prices rose dramatically. This was during the midst of a severe depression. Who out of all the experts predicted this? The law of averages would suggest that some would have predicted something similar to this. But for each 'expert' that would have predicted this (by chance), there would have been many more who would not have. Human nature is such that those who did 'predict' this are much more likely to make themselves known than those who 'predicted' something very different.

Lack of Trust

I am not sure whether this should be a valid reason for not taking financial advice. For instance, I have not always understood the costs associated with getting my car serviced. I have not always been convinced that various parts that have been replaced needed to be when the garage said they did. This lack of trust has nevertheless not stopped me from having my car serviced in the future. I just felt that I had to be careful where I chose to go.

In areas where specialist knowledge or skills are needed, trust is paramount. This is very true where financial advice is concerned.

I believe that many of us know of instances where advisers have not acted in a client's best interests. Lack of trust can therefore be sometimes justified. Sometimes it can be a little harsh. After all, we cannot be liable for world events and how they impact on the value of your investments, for instance.

** * * * * * **

I am hopeful that this book will get across that there are some occasions where advice is extremely valuable. The idea of avoiding advice at all costs because of previous experience will not serve you well moving forward. It is like avoiding getting married again because your previous husband or wife was a pig. This does not mean that your next adviser (or spouse) will be.

CHAPTER 1

YOUR OBJECTIVES AND NEEDS

WHAT ARE MY OBJECTIVES?

I would consider this the most important chapter in this book. We should all know what the objectives are when taking out a financial plan of any description.

There is a quote by Steven Covey (author of "The 7 Habits of Highly Successful People") – "Begin with the end in mind". In other words:

- What is it you want to ultimately achieve?
- What are your goals in life and how do you aim to achieve them?

For the purposes of this book:

■ What part will money play in helping you achieve them?

For instance, nobody should want a pension. I believe what people really want is a long and prosperous retirement. You could take this a stage further and say that you want to be financially secure in retirement and maintain the same standard of living in retirement as you enjoy now. In many cases, retirement planning can mean one or a number of pension plans. It could also mean other assets that you have accumulated. Many of you may look upon the value of your property as a way of providing for your retirement. A pension plan is a product not an objective. It is merely a tax efficient way of saving towards that particular objective.

Equally, nobody should want life cover. The objective in this instance is to help protect your loved ones against the financial impact of your premature death. This comes under the heading of 'risk management'. An example here would be that you may want your children to have the best education and start in life. Your plan/goal, in this instance, would be to provide financially to help see this through. Risk management covers the 'what if?' scenarios. With financial planning, it tries to address those rare, unforeseen events that could ruin your plans.

The above 2 examples may appear basic but I don't believe that people think sufficiently enough about their objectives. In the past, the emphasis has been in buying (or being sold) financial products.

Many accumulate a number of policies. In some cases, they are paying regular amounts and they may have even forgotten what benefits these plans provide. This is where a plan or product was originally sold and not reviewed to ensure that it was still relevant. An annual review should serve as a reminder of what the objectives were and whether the plans or policies you hold still go to serve that objective.

WHY SHOULD I SAVE?

The future will come whether you plan for it or not. Will you have the future you have planned for?

Once you have decided what your future should look like and how you want your life to be, it is then a matter of what part money can play in this.

Most milestones have a financial component to them. Some examples are as follows:

- House purchase.
- Car purchase.
- Become financially independent.
- Retirement fund.
- Further education for children (or even grandchildren).
- Buy a holiday home.
- A special holiday or trip.

This list is by no means exhaustive and there may be other examples that are personal to you.

For some of you, there may be the idea of buying a holiday home in France, for example. Without a plan in place which covers at least the financing of this, it may not happen. In order to bring this dream to life, you need to specify a target date for this to be achieved. This date would be based mainly on your desire but, in order for this to be realistic, it should also be based on the financial reality of being able to afford it. A plan needn't be rigid. Circumstances change and your objectives should be reviewed and amended where necessary.

Rather than save for capital items, some of you would look towards borrowing the funds needed. As a direct result of the borrowing culture, it has recently become harder to find credit. Whereas 100% mortgages were readily available, it is not unusual to see deposits of 10%/15% of the purchase price being needed. If you therefore want to buy a house, it would probably be a good idea to start saving. That is unless you are lucky enough to have the money given to you. Equally, you also have a slight chance of winning the lottery.

It may not be possible to borrow funds to finance some items on your wish list. I would highlight becoming financially secure and retirement as two areas where borrowing is not practical.

Although retirement planning has a section of its own (Chapter 4), this is one area in particular where I feel many fail to plan adequately enough. Those fortunate to be in good final salary/defined benefit schemes will not have to do as much planning as others. For many, retirement planning consists of putting some money into a personal pension and hoping for the best. Where a defined contribution company arrangement is offered, the terms can be set by the criteria for joining the scheme. For instance, if you are required to contribute 4% of your pay to be a member of the pension scheme, you may feel as though that is all you need to contribute and that will be enough to obtain a decent retirement income. The reality is that it is unlikely to be enough. Some do not contribute to a pension at all in the belief that they can use their home as a pension fund or that the State will provide.

Retirement planning also dovetails into other parts of your financial planning. For instance, you may like to go on one or more holidays each year. If you do not set aside sufficient funds for your retirement, this lifestyle could be put in jeopardy simply because you no longer have the money to continue to fund the lifestyle you currently enjoy. Something has to go.

SHOULD I BORROW IN ORDER TO ACHIEVE MY GOALS?

Debt is bad. Savings are good. This being said, the vast majority of us cannot hope to buy some of our most expensive capital items without a loan. A mortgage is the most typical of these. More home owners have a mortgage than do not.

It is obvious to say that the more borrowing you have, the more interest you pay. The more you have to pay back will ultimately lead to less money you will have available to spend or save in other areas.

When debt is out of proportion in relation to your income or assets, it can cripple you financially. You may have the home of your dreams but if most of your income is taken up with mortgage repayments, this may be at the cost of other financial goals.

A website I have come across where you can test whether you are too much in debt is: www.jpmorgan.realise.com/obesityscale.

You may wish to visit this website and check whether your level of debt should be of concern to you.

WHY SHOULD I PUT PROTECTION IN PLACE?

Protection is used to cater for the 'what if' scenarios and how they could interfere with your financial goals. This is the management of risk.

Home/property insurance and car insurance are typical examples of risk management. Other examples could include an extended warranty to cover the breakdown of an electrical item. The breakdown of a household appliance would set you back possibly by a few hundred pounds. I would suggest, however, that the loss of the income of a major earner would be much more financially devastating.

A more common use of personal protection would be in connection with a property purchase. A life cover plan is often used as a way of repaying a mortgage in the event of premature death. A critical illness plan and/or even an income protection plan could also be added to provide extra cover against serious illness (See Chapter 3).

There are many instances where protection cover is needed. Many parents would want their children to benefit from the same standard of living and education even if they weren't around to see it. They may be saving for future events such as their children's education. A protection plan is also likely to be needed to prepare for those disastrous events that can devastate families such as severe illness resulting in loss of income and even death.

In short, protection plans are intended for rare events that have a large financial impact. Insurance effectively pools together all the premiums to pay for those unfortunate to be devastated by such rare events.

It would be foolhardy to put money aside in order to buy a replacement home in case your existing one burns down. Most people wouldn't even think of not insuring their valuable possessions. And yet, it is those events affecting life and health that can have an even greater financial impact.

An extended warranty for electrical goods, for example, could be put in the category of something that could be considered of limited financial impact. I would also suggest that the possibility of electrical goods breaking down is not that rare an event. I have therefore come to the conclusion that these types of plans are sold more often than they are purchased. Maybe that is true of most protection plans. Often, it is the adviser (or salesperson) that emphasises the potential problem before recommending a solution.

WHY DO I NEED A CASH RESERVE?

Too many people live from one day to the next. They rarely put their efforts into setting money aside for the future let alone building up a cash reserve. The consequence of this is that most people do not have a cash reserve – but ideally they should.

A cash reserve is sometimes referred to as an emergency fund. These are usually funds that are specifically earmarked for an emergency such as the loss of a job. This would be to cover such items where insurance would not be typically available.

The value of your reserve fund could be based on a multiple of your income. This could be, say, 6 months' pay. It could be more or less than this. Ideally, the fund should be sufficient to cover expenses incurred between jobs.

An emergency fund is effectively a 'safety net' to help you cope with most financial events that come along. It provides many with the 'peace of mind' that they will be able to cope (financially) with what life sometimes throws at us.

WHY DO I NEED TO PRIORITISE?

There may be a number of items on your wish list. Whether you can achieve all of these, or just some for now, will depend on your finances.

If you currently live in rented accommodation and earn, say, £10,000 a year, it may be impractical to plan to save towards a Rolls Royce, a speedboat and a holiday home in Miami. Although this is an extreme example, it is intended to illustrate that you need to prioritise which of your financial objectives/goals take precedence.

This is not to say you should not still desire some of the finer things that life has to offer. The point is that you may not be able to achieve all of these objectives, it is then a matter of prioritisation.

The same is true of your protection requirements. Although you may wish to protect against premature death and serious illness as well as provide protection for your income, the total cost for full protection maybe more than you would allow for in your budget. It then becomes a matter of whether you obtain full cover in just some of these important areas or whether you settle for partial cover. This could include, for example, just protecting your mortgage.

DO YOU BUY INSURANCE PLANS OR ARE THEY SOLD TO YOU?

There is evidence to show that most protection plans are sold rather than purchased. This could be due to the persuasiveness of the adviser. A good, scrupulous adviser will point out the need for cover and explain how much cover is required. It is the advice that is valued rather than the actual product. This same level of expertise is seldom found in price comparison websites or, indeed, with many other direct providers of life assurance and protection plans.

An example of where interaction with a professional is paramount is with Will planning. Most people I meet see a need to make a Will. That's the easy part. The next and most important step, however, is actually getting around to doing something about it. Without the interaction with another professional, this may never happen.

There are many instances where a little encouragement is needed in order to complete your goals. Retirement planning is one such example of this. The general public often requires help in knowing how much to save towards their retirement. Encouragement is often needed to start saving towards your retirement. After all, there is never a good time to save. There are always other things to spend your money on which may appear more of a priority at the time. Car purchase, house purchase, marriage, child birth are just some examples where there is a demand on your finances. It is all too easy to concentrate too much on these areas and neglect longer term objectives such as planning for your retirement.

Where life cover and protection products are purchased, the main emphasis is often on cost rather than the relevance of the cover. Price comparison websites, by their very nature, aim at looking for the cheapest form of cover. Whether this will be sufficient cover for your requirements is another matter.

SHOULD MY PLANS BE REVIEWED REGULARLY?

Question yourself as to why, several years ago, you may have taken out life cover that provides a payment on death, of say £25,000. Have your circumstances changed since then? Is that cover still needed? Is it enough?

My experience is that many clients take out policies, get into the habit of paying monthly premiums and forget about them. This isn't always the case but it happens far too often. Some get so used to paying the regular monthly direct debit that they never re-visit as to what the original purpose was for.

With pension plans, many are content with the fact that they have a pension rather than looking at what benefits they expect to receive. The emphasis can be on how much is contributed rather than on how much they will receive when they come to retire. Again, this isn't always the case.

Many over-estimate the value of the plans they have. Inflation naturally reduces the value of savings/investments as well as the value of life cover as time passes by. This is a main reason why the need for regular reviews is required.

Putting together a plan is a significant step in achieving your long term objectives. An annual review will provide the discipline of ensuring you remain on track.

A plan needn't be rigid. Your goals may change in which case your financial plan would need to be adapted to cope with this. Your circumstances may change. An inheritance, divorce, death, the loss of a job or any significant life changing event can advance or put back the timing of your objectives. A periodic review of your financial plan would deal with these changes.

MAIN POINTS TO CONSIDER

✓ It is what you need money for rather than money itself that is important.

✓ Know what your objectives are and put a plan in place.

✓ Prioritise what is most important to you as you are unlikely to be financially able to do everything you want to.

✓ Use protection plans to help guard financially against potentially devastating events.

✓ Review your plans regularly to ensure you remain on target. Things change. Seldom do circumstances remain the same.

FINAL THOUGHT

Money can be, in effect, just paper, worthless metal or numbers that appear on a bank statement. It can be a medium of exchange and/or a store of wealth. It is the goods or services you can exchange money for (now and in the future) that is the most important thing and not the money itself.

CHAPTER 2

LIFE COVER

WHY IS LIFE COVER NEEDED?

I have found it a little difficult to understand that many material possessions are covered against loss, damage or theft and yet lives are not always insured, as a matter of course.

Many insure their houses – the contents as well as the buildings. Even though it is the law to insure your car, many go above the basic need of 'third party' cover and insure on a fully comprehensive basis. You may even select cover to protect an electrical appliance

It is true that people are living longer. The chances of a male dying before age 65 are comparatively rare. Nevertheless, you still stand a greater chance of dying than winning the jackpot prize in the National Lottery. Based on these facts, it is difficult to understand why the main emphasis could be to buy lottery tickets in preference to putting an adequate level of life cover in place.

I have come across many instances where the financial impact of death has been devastating. You may know of situations too. The loved ones left behind are the ones that have to make do.

Whilst many parents want the best for their children, the impression they give is that this is only when they are alive. I am sure this is not the case. Some parents may put money aside to fund their children's education, for example. Nevertheless, a simple low cost life cover plan can run alongside a savings plan to ensure that your loved ones still have enough funds to fulfil their further education even in the event of your premature death.

There are so many priorities in life that appear to take precedence over life cover. Holidays, repaying a mortgage, saving towards a child's future are all examples. And yet the same people who believe it is an unnecessary expense would indulge in expenditure such as buying lottery tickets (gambling) and other social expenses such as drinking and smoking.

To protect your family against the financial impact of your death is not as expensive as you may think.

WHAT ARE THE MAIN REASONS FOR TAKING OUT COVER?

The main reasons are usually as follows:

- To repay borrowing such as a mortgage.
- To replace an income to be payable to your dependents in the event of death.
- To pay for child care costs.

Life cover is particularly important in instances where there are dependents who would suffer financially in the event of death of a major earner within the relationship. This is particularly true where children are involved as their future is affected by any financial hardship that the family unit would suffer.

Both adults in a relationship may be financially inter-dependent in order to maintain their chosen lifestyle. In that instance, life cover may be appropriate for both parties in order to protect each other.

Other reasons for life cover may include:

- To pay a potential Inheritance Tax (IHT) bill.
- To pay for funeral costs.

There are steps that can be taken to reduce or eliminate any potential Inheritance Tax liability. These are not to be covered in this chapter. Where there remains an outstanding liability, one way to alleviate the financial impact of this tax is to put in place cover of an amount sufficient to pay the tax.

The use of life cover to pay for funeral costs is more of a generational thing. To illustrate this, my grandmother was particularly concerned that none of her children should have to pay for her funeral. My mother takes a different view. She is of the opinion that there are plenty of funds within her Estate to cover any such costs.

In the vast majority of cases, **life cover should be written in trust**. This is for 2 main reasons:

- To ensure the proceeds are paid directly to the beneficiaries without the need for Grant of Probate/Letters of Administration. This ensures that the monies are paid directly to those intended with the minimum of delay.
- To prevent the funds being brought within your Estate and being assessed for Inheritance Tax.

Life cover is paid out free of tax in most instances.

SHOULD MY COVER BE REVIEWED?

Like most things in life, nothing stays the same.

- Have your circumstances changed since the cover was originally taken out?

- Is the level of cover still appropriate? Should this be increased? Is cover still needed?

- Is the existing cover written in trust? Should it be?

- Are the premiums too expensive? Are there now more cost effective options?

Far too often, I see cases where life cover was put in force several years ago and the plans have not been reviewed since. In such cases, the policyholder forgets how much cover they have. They habitually continue to pay the premiums via direct debit and forget what the objectives were in taking out the policy.

It must be emphasised that this isn't true in every instance. It just happens far too often (in my opinion).

WHAT DIFFERENT TYPES OF LIFE COVER ARE THERE?

There are mainly two types of life cover plans available:

- Term assurance
- Whole of life

Historically, you may also have endowment plans or pension term assurance plans in place.

Term assurance   This is where cover is put in place for a specified period of time.

Whole of life   This is where cover is put in place for an indefinite period.

WHAT ARE THE MAIN REASONS FOR TERM ASSURANCE?

This is where cover is required for a specific period of time. If cover is required to protect your children until they are no longer dependent on you, you may want the end-term to coincide with the youngest's 18th or even 21st birthday.

If it is your partner or spouse who is dependent and who the cover is aimed at, you may want the end date to coincide with your chosen retirement date.

A term assurance plan is also appropriate to run alongside a loan such as a mortgage. The term of the cover should coincide with the term of the loan.

Although there is an argument why a whole of life policy could be used in place of a term assurance plan, this should be the exception rather than the rule.

Term assurance is often the most cost effective way of providing life cover. The premiums can be guaranteed from the outset based on the period that the cover is required.

A basic term assurance can have other features as follows:

■ It can increase each year – the idea would be for the level of cover to keep pace with inflation and maintain the true value.

■ It can decrease each year – this would be where cover was intended to repay a loan that was gradually being repaid. Another example would be where cover is used to protect a family. A lesser sum assured could be needed as the younger family members become less dependent.

■ Cover could be renewable – this is where a defined period is agreed from the outset but with the option of renewing the plan at the end of that initial period. This allows for the possibility of extending cover **without** the need for further medical underwriting.

■ The plan could be converted into another plan such as a whole of life plan providing this option was exercised before the end of the initial term.

WHAT ARE THE CIRCUMSTANCES WHERE WHOLE OF LIFE (INDEFINITE) COVER IS NEEDED?

This is usually where the cover is required on death, whenever that ultimately turns out to be. The main two examples of where this type of cover is most appropriate are:

- To pay an Inheritance Tax (IHT) bill.
- To pay for funeral costs.

Term assurance is not really appropriate in either of these instances as although we know we will die, we don't necessarily know when. A term cannot therefore be determined from the outset.

Although a whole of life plan is intended as life cover, there is an element of investment that forms a feature of this type of policy. I have seen instances where this type of plan has been promoted as an investment. This shouldn't have happened as the main purpose for a whole of life plan is as a way of providing life cover.

Care should be taken regarding the type of whole of life cover that is selected. A maximum cover plan, for instance, may start out by being competitive on cost. Once the initial review, in 5 or 10 years, has taken place it is likely that the cost will significantly increase in order to maintain the initial level of cover for a further period.

IS THE CHEAPEST COVER THE BEST?

Where term assurance life cover is concerned, the answer is usually – YES. For other types of life cover such as 'whole of life', the answer isn't as straightforward.

When recommending term assurance life cover, I always look for the lowest *guaranteed* premium as the start point. This is where the premiums are guaranteed through the term required. Where premiums are reviewed, the worry is that the premiums are likely to be reviewed upwards. I have been assured by some life companies that this needn't be the case. Nevertheless, a guaranteed premium will ensure that this would not happen.

Many life companies offer additional benefits such as payment upon diagnosis of a terminal illness. In this scenario, if you were to have been diagnosed as having less than 12 months to live, the life company would pay out on this diagnosis rather than waiting until death.

Generally speaking, there is nothing contentious with regards to life cover claims – if you die, the sum assured is paid out. Providing that cover is through a reputable, well established company there should be no problem. It is also appropriate to point out that deliberate non disclosure or false disclosure of medical details when completing the proposal form could affect a claim.

If other features of a term assurance plan are required such as renewable cover, then the cost of premiums may not be the most determinant factor.

Please take care with regards to accidental death cover types of insurance. Whilst the premiums are usually very cheap, there is a reason for this. This type of plan usually only pays out in the event of death as a result of an accident. Whilst this can happen, it is a very rare occurrence. You are much more likely to die of cancer or a heart attack than in a plane crash or being run over by a bus, for example.

The underwriting connected with life cover reminds me of the saying regarding bankers: "A banker will lend you an umbrella when it is sunny but ask you for it back when it starts raining". If you are well, you should have little difficulty in obtaining life cover. If you have serious health issues, there will be problems. The trick with life cover is therefore to have it in place **before** your health deteriorates. This is because when the time comes where it may be needed, you may be unlikely to be granted cover. And even if cover was granted, it is likely to be very costly.

IS ADVICE REALLY REQUIRED WHERE LIFE COVER IS INVOLVED?

Historically, life cover has been sold and not bought. It has been the discussions with a financial adviser or life assurance salesman that has led to a life policy being put in force.

More recently, the increased use of the internet and price comparison websites has led to the public being able to view the most competitive rates available. Even the supermarkets are getting in on the act. You only have to be in the checkout queue to experience the range of financial services that the supermarkets are offering these days. This includes life cover.

Where life cover is viewed as a product to be purchased, it is difficult to see why the services of an adviser would be needed. After all, the advice costs (commission) can be stripped out of the product when this is offered directly to the consumer. This undoubtedly reduces the cost/premium.

Ask yourself this question? – Am I taking out this cover because it is cheap or because it is the cover I require to provide the protection I need?

A skilled adviser can discuss what your priorities are and advise as to the level and type of cover that is required. A proper 'needs analysis' can be completed. Other types of life cover could be recommended rather than just straight term assurance life cover. An example I would use would be Family Income Benefit.

WHAT IS FAMILY INCOME BENEFIT?

This is a form of decreasing term assurance that pays an amount each year as opposed to a lump sum. This is designed specifically to replace income.

An ideal situation where this type of cover is needed is to replace your income for the ultimate benefit of your children. A typical life cover plan will pay a lump sum. This can be invested with the intention of replacing the income that was lost from the wage earner. The same amount is however payable at the beginning of the term, when the child is young, compared with the end of the term, when the child is likely to be less dependent.

Let us look at an example where a replacement income of, say, £20,000 per annum is required. The period required could be until the child is 21 years old. The total potential pay-out is £420,000 (£20,000 x 21 years). The risk to the provider/insurance company lessens as the child gets older. This is because as the remaining term gets shorter, the amount the provider can pay out effectively reduces, as the plan reaches its end date.

The end result is that this type of cover can be obtained at a lower cost compared with a term assurance plan that would provide the full £420,000 over the 21 years.

A Family Income Benefit plan is not suitable for the purposes of repaying borrowing where a lump sum is needed to repay the outstanding balance. It is, however, suitable for the example used above and should be considered in those situations.

MAIN POINTS TO CONSIDER

✓ The loss of an income can be more financially devastating than the loss of an asset such as a car.

✓ Life cover is relatively inexpensive whereas the financial impact of the death of a breadwinner can be devastating.

✓ Death is certain. It is just a matter of when.

✓ There are different types of life cover - each suitable for different circumstances.

✓ In most situations, life cover should be written in trust.

✓ Review your plans regularly to ensure you continue to have the right type and level of cover.

FINAL THOUGHTS

- What financial impact would there be to my family if I died?

- Would I still be able to enjoy the lifestyle (including holidays) I currently do?

- Would my children still have the same start in life?

- What would be payable in the event of my death (if anything)?

- Would my dependants be able to live on this together with any savings they would have?

If your answers to these questions concern you, you need to take action sooner rather than later. Alternatively, if you are not sure about the answers, you may need help or advice.

CHAPTER 3

CRITICAL ILLNESS, PERMANENT HEALTH INSURANCE, ACCIDENT & SICKNESS COVER

This chapter nicely follows on from 'Chapter 2 – Life Cover'.

The difference here is that these types of cover are designed to pay out in the event of illness rather than death. Apart from that, the three types of plan are different. In most cases, they can be combined with a life cover so that a payment is made either in the event of illness and/or death.

WHY IS ILLNESS COVER REQUIRED?

The Office for National Statistics reveals figures that show that you are 5 times more likely to suffer a serious/critical illness than die, prior to the age of 65.

Long term illness can, nevertheless, have just as major a financial impact as death. Whereas death is final, illness can be recoverable. Equally, you may not recover sufficiently enough to regain your full earnings capacity. Even if you do resume your normal daily duties, there could be a period of time where you are off work whilst you recover.

Many employers will pay you if you are off work ill. Your contract of employment is a good place to look to see what the terms are. For example, you may receive full pay for, say, 4 weeks and then just be entitled to any state benefits after then. Other employers may pay for a longer period and then reduce the pay down to half pay after, say, one month. If you are not sure what benefits you would receive, then check.

For those who work for themselves or where the employment terms are not so generous, it is a matter of either relying on what the state would provide or putting in place your own cover.

Throughout this chapter we will look at the features of the main types of cover there are. We will also look at the similarities as well as the differences with regards to the types of illness protection there is. You should then have more of an idea of what type of plan you would need or whether you already have the right type of plan to suit your circumstances.

WHAT IS CRITICAL ILLNESS COVER?

This type of cover is similar to life cover insofar as a lump sum is payable. A premium is also paid and a term is agreed at the outset. The difference is that the lump sum/sum assured is paid on the diagnosis of a critical illness. In most cases, you would have to survive the illness/event for a period that may be up to 30 days before the sum assured is paid out. This is why critical illness cover is often combined with a life cover plan in order to ensure that it pays out even if you don't survive this period. This is often referred to as integrated critical illness cover.

Medical advances mean that the chances of you surviving a critical illness are increasing all the time. For instance, 80% of those diagnosed with breast cancer are still alive 5 years later on. This wasn't the prognosis 30 to 40 years ago.

Whereas life cover pays out on death in the overwhelming majority of instances, the claims history relating to critical illness cover is more chequered. Where medical issues are concerned, it is the non-disclosure of certain conditions that can lead to non-payment. It is also the definition of the critical illness that can cause arguments between the claimant and the provider. Those of us who are not as medically aware may believe that being diagnosed with cancer or a heart attack should mean that they are eligible to claim. The problem is that not all cancers are the same. The insurers are likely to state what exclusions there are from the very outset. With a heart attack, this term can sometimes be used loosely to describe a range of other heart conditions, some of which may not be covered. Many believe that their plan covers them for these eventualities. They may not. The wording of the definitions is crucial. Unfortunately, very few will look closely at these definitions until such time as when looking at submitting a claim. This can be the cause of complaints as a policyholder may think they are covered only to find out they are not when their claim is declined.

It is for the above reasons that not all critical illness plans are the same.

WHAT CONDITIONS ARE COVERED?

The Association of British Insurers (ABI) has issued a Statement of Best Practice for Critical Illness Cover. Prior to then there were a specified number of core conditions that were, and still are, usually covered in most critical illness policies. These were as follows:

- Cancer
- Heart attack
- Kidney failure
- Stroke (resulting in permanent symptoms)
- Multiple sclerosis

- Major organ transplant
- Coronary artery bypass.

There are a number of further conditions that are also commonly covered but are not always. These are listed below:

- Aorta graft surgery
- Benign brain tumour
- Blindness (permanent and irreversible)
- Coma
- Deafness (permanent and irreversible)
- Heart valve replacement
- Loss of limb
- Loss of speech
- Motor neurone disease
- Paralysis/paraplegia
- Parkinson's disease
- Terminal illness
- Third degree burns.

An insurer/provider may choose to go further in a bid to gain a competitive advantage by adding further conditions. These may include Alzheimer's disease, liver failure, rheumatoid arthritis and/or severe lung disease. Before you go looking through your policy to see if 'aplastic anaemia' is covered, for example, it is probably an appropriate time to mention that over half the critical illness claims are for cancer. Number two in the claims is heart attack although this is much more prevalent with males than females. Way behind in the list of claims comes a stroke, multiple sclerosis and benign brain tumour.

Most of the conditions listed outside of the core conditions represent a very small proportion of claims. Looking at the claims recorded for 2008-2010 for critical illness, the top 5 illnesses as mentioned above represents over 88% of the total claims.

They were as follows:

- Cancer – 65.11%
- Heart attack – 9.74%
- Stroke – 6.32%
- Multiple sclerosis – 5.14%
- Benign brain tumour – 2.28%

All insurers issue comprehensive lists of what conditions are covered. They also go into detail of what traits signify a claim and, just as importantly, what doesn't.

The ABI has also published industry standard definitions for the plan exclusions most commonly used. The standard exclusions for many illnesses are as follows:

- Alcohol or drug abuse
- Criminal acts
- Self-inflicted injury
- Act of war or rebellion.

Full details are contained in the ABI Statement of Best Practice for Critical Illness cover.

WILL CRITICAL ILLNESS COVER PROTECT ME IN ALL CIRCUMSTANCES?

The straightforward answer to this is NO! If you cannot work due to any condition that is not listed, no legitimate claim can be made.

To illustrate this, I will tell you a true story of a lady who was involved in a car crash. For a period of time, she was in a bad way. She was off work for over 6 months and has never made a full recovery. She broke many bones in her body including one arm, both legs and her pelvis. There were a number of internal injuries. We scoured through the critical illness policy definitions and found that there was no basis for a claim.

The blind spot with most critical illness policies is where there are issues such as joint, ligament, bone and back problems or even stress. These conditions can mean that you may no longer be able to carry out your normal day to day duties, and yet a claim under a critical illness plan would not be valid.

In other words, your income may have shrunk due to you being off work for a length of time. Your ability to provide for your family and repay borrowing such as your mortgage would be severely compromised. If it is this scenario that concerns you the most, then a Permanent Health Insurance (PHI)/ Income replacement plan is likely to be a better option for you.

WHAT IS PERMANENT HEALTH INSURANCE (PHI)?

This is also known as Income Protection. This type of insurance is designed to replace your income in the event of you not being able to work due to illness or accident.

It is because some occupations are more hazardous than others that the calculation for the cost of cover is determined by your occupation. This is in addition to the usual factors such as the amount of cover, health, age, sex and length of cover. Any hazardous pastimes would also be taken into consideration.

A successful claim will result in a proportion of your income being paid out on a monthly basis as opposed to a lump sum. There are maximum limits that are placed on this type of cover. This is because the intention is for you not to profit from being off work ill.

The reason it is called 'Permanent' Health Insurance is because once the plan is in force, it cannot be cancelled by the provider. In other words, a term will be selected from the outset. A typical period would be for the cover to end at the age you plan to retire (e.g. age 65). Any claim would therefore result in the benefits being payable every month until any of the following:

- The selected age/term agreed at the outset
- Retirement
- Death
- Recovery.

WHAT CONDITIONS ARE COVERED?

Anything that affects you not being able to work can result in a claim. This is where there is a fundamental difference from critical illness cover where the precise wording of the illness is crucial. That being said, there are again different types of cover out there.

I would differentiate between three different standards in respect of the definition of incapacity. These can be summarised as follows:

- Own occupation
- Any suited occupation
- Any occupation.

Without going into too much detail, the most robust of the above definitions is 'own occupation'. In short, anything that stops you doing your day-to-day duties will result in a claim. End of.

The weakest of the definitions is 'any occupation'. What this refers to is that a claim will only be sanctioned if your illness/accident prevents you from working in any capacity. An example of this would be if an illness prevented you performing, say, brain surgery but you were still able to work as a car park attendant. A claim may not be successful under the 'any occupation' definition. That is because you can still work. For that example (and most others), I would strongly suggest and recommend the 'own occupation' definition.

WHAT OTHER FACTORS SHOULD I BE AWARE OF?

The medical underwriting for life cover and critical illness cover is such that you are either covered or not. With PHI, this is not necessarily as straightforward. For instance, you may have a history of back problems. Rather than cover being declined outright, the insurer may treat the back problems as a pre-existing medical condition and exclude this from cover. In other words, you would be covered for all conditions except if it was the back problem that prevented you from working. This is similar to how private medical insurance is underwritten.

Another area to consider is the deferred period. With life cover, the claim should ideally be settled immediately with the minimum of delay. With critical illness, there can be a period of up to 30 days whereby you would be required to survive for that period before a claim would be considered. For PHI, this is slightly different. A deferred period is agreed at the start of the cover. This would be for a minimum of 4 weeks. This prevents claims for minor ailments or injuries. The deferment period should, ideally, be aligned with the period your employer will pay you for being off work. For instance, if your employer pays you for up to 3 months full pay due to illness, a deferment period of 13 weeks would be appropriate.

The longer the deferment period, the lower the cost. Some of you may be comfortable with knowing you would be financially OK to be able to survive without any income for 3 to 6 months. Any longer would cause problems. A deferment period of 13 to 26 weeks would provide cover in those circumstances. This would give you the peace of mind knowing you and your family would cope with the otherwise financial hardship.

WILL PHI COVER PROTECT ME IN ALL CIRCUMSTANCES?

Not all types of PHI plans are the same. Care should be taken with regards to the wording and the definition of incapacity. This was illustrated as above. There are some occupations (e.g. Deep sea diving) where it can be difficult to get cover.

The most robust PHI plan with an 'own occupation' definition should provide cover for the vast majority of workers. The area I would suggest that isn't covered by a stand-alone PHI plan is where illness occurs and there is little or no chance of recovery. In this scenario, a life cover and/or critical illness plan would fill this potential gap.

To emphasis this point further, a successful critical illness claim would result in a lump sum being payable that would be designed to repay a loan such as a mortgage. A successful PHI claim, on the other hand, would be intended to replace your income so that you could continue to meet your loan/mortgage repayments as well as the majority of other living costs.

WHAT IS ACCIDENT AND SICKNESS COVER?

This is very similar to income protection/Permanent Health Insurance cover (PHI). This is because it is designed to replace income in the event of accident or sickness. This type of cover is usually promoted as a way of protecting your mortgage repayments and should be much less expensive than PHI.

Accident and sickness cover is often combined with unemployment cover thus providing extra protection should you lose your job due to unforeseen circumstances such as redundancy. These types of plans are referred to as ASU (accident, sickness and unemployment) plans.

WHAT CONDITIONS ARE COVERED AND WHAT FACTORS SHOULD I BE AWARE OF?

There is very little difference with accident and sickness cover compared with PHI insofar as what is covered. As with PHI, pre-existing medical conditions are usually excluded from the plan.

There are however two major differences as follows:

- The deferred or waiting period is usually a standard 30 days. There is no choice with this. With PHI, you can select the deferred period between 4 weeks and sometimes up to 104 weeks (2 years).
- There is a maximum period of payment. This is usually 12 months but could be for a longer period such as 2 years. Whereas PHI is guaranteed to pay out until the pre-selected date of expiry, this is not the case with accident and sickness

cover. The end result is that because this cover is not as all encompassing as PHI, the costs are significantly lower.

You would usually find this type of plan connected with taking out a mortgage policy.

WILL ACCIDENT AND SICKNESS COVER PLANS PROTECT ME IN ALL CIRCUMSTANCES?

There aren't any separate definitions with regards to own occupation or any occupation with accident & sickness policies. The underwriting process is, as a result, usually much more straightforward.

The main problem with this type of cover compared with PHI plans are that they only pay out for a limited period of time (usually 1 to 2 years). For anyone suffering financial hardship due to long-term illness or injury, these plans only offer temporary respite.

As with PHI, accident & sickness plans can be coupled with life cover and/or critical illness cover with the aim of providing a more all-round protection package.

MAIN POINTS TO CONSIDER

✓ Long term illness can have just as detrimental effect on your finances as would premature death.

✓ You are more likely to suffer a serious illness and survive (before the age of 65) than to die.

✓ Over half the claims under a critical illness cover are for cancer.

✓ Income protection plans cover long term absences including back and joint problems whereas these conditions are not covered under a critical illness plan.

✓ For all round cover, you may need more than one plan.

✓ Review your plans regularly to ensure you continue to have the right level of cover as well as the most appropriate type of cover.

FINAL THOUGHTS

■ What financial impact would there be to my family if I were unable to work as a result of illness or accident?

■ What benefits would I receive from the State in the event of illness/accident?

■ For how long would my employer pay me if I couldn't work as a result of illness/accident?

■ What (if anything) would my employer pay me if I couldn't work as a result of illness/accident?

■ What am I specifically covered for with my existing policies?

If your answers to these questions worry you, then you need to take action. Alternatively, if you are uncertain about the answers, you may need help or advice.

CHAPTER 4

RETIREMENT PLANNING

WHY SAVE FOR YOUR RETIREMENT?

Retirement planning is a way of ensuring that you have sufficient funds available to do the things that you want to when you retire from working.

It is vital to put funds aside in order to avoid long-term poverty in old age.

The Association of British Insurers' (ABI) Savings and Protection survey in 2009 demonstrates that the lack of retirement planning is a serious problem. Nearly half (42%) of the UK workforce face financial problems in retirement. A further 13% are saving at levels unlikely to provide an adequate income. A further 30% are saving NOTHING towards their retirement. This leaves just 15% who can positively look forward to their retirement without worrying too much about money.

The following statistics demonstrate just how serious the problem is:

- 19% of adults hope to improve their standard of living in retirement by winning the lottery.
- 30% of households have no savings, home contents insurance, or a private pension.

[Friends Provident Corporate Responsibility Report 2008]

People are living longer!

After you retire, there is every chance you will live half the number of years again that you have been working. On average, the majority of UK residents could realistically expect to live over 20 years (depending on health, diet and exercise). In order to maintain the same lifestyle that you have become accustomed to, you will have to accumulate a significant fund. This should be of a value to last you for what should be a long period of time.

The 2001 census revealed that there were 11 million people over the age of 65 in the UK. That represents 18.6% of the total population. If a male retires at age 65, he can expect to live a further 16.9 years (on average). For women, it is a further 19.7 years. (Source: Office for National Statistics February 2008). We all know of those who live longer. It used to be a very rare event for people to live to the age of 100. It is not as rare as it used to be.

As at the 2012/2013 tax year, the Basic State Pension is just over £5,500 per annum or £107 per week. Even the authorities accept that this is not sufficient to live on, hence the need to consider additional ways to fund your retirement.

DO YOU WANT TO ENJOY YOUR RETIREMENT OR JUST SURVIVE?

I would suggest to everyone that they complete the simple weekly planner below giving details of what they wish to do during a typical week when they retire. This should ideally be done as a joint exercise with your partner. I have done this in the past as part of a pre-retirement seminar. It never ceases to amaze me how seldom couples discuss with each other how they wish to spend their retirement.

WEEKLY PLANNER

	MONDAY	TUESDAY	WEDNESDAY	THURSDAY	FRIDAY	SATURDAY	SUNDAY
MORNING							
AFTERNOON							
EVENING							

The next stage is to cost it out.

WEEKLY PLANNER SHOWING COSTS

	MONDAY	TUESDAY	WEDNESDAY	THURSDAY	FRIDAY	SATURDAY	SUNDAY
MORNING	(£	(£)	(£)	(£)	(£)	(£)	(£)
AFTERNOON	(£	(£)	(£)	(£)	(£)	(£)	(£)
EVENING	(£	(£)	(£)	(£)	(£)	(£)	(£)

I am often told by clients that they will need less money when they retire. They believe this to be the case because:

- Kids should be off their hands.
- The mortgage should have been repaid.

What many fail to take into account is the extra costs associated with living at home. The energy bills will be higher as you will undoubtedly spend more time at home, particularly during the winter months. If you want to go on holiday or on trips out, for instance, this also costs. To demonstrate this point, many spend more money on Saturdays and Sundays compared with the rest of the week. When you retire, every day is effectively a Saturday and Sunday.

Retirement is often referred to as the 'longest holiday of your life'. How good a time you have on this 'holiday' will depend on factors such as your health. Nevertheless, the amount of money you have to spend will also be a significant factor.

WHAT ARE PENSIONS?

A pension is basically a long term savings plan. There are tax relief benefits in contributing to a pension plan. Without such tax reliefs, there would be little advantage in contributing to a pension as opposed to other savings plans such as ISAs or even putting funds in the bank.

In the interests of simplicity, I will illustrate the features of a defined contribution/money purchase arrangement as opposed to a defined benefit/final salary scheme.

Pensions can be perceived as being complicated. I would suggest that this is because the savings part (accumulation) is amalgamated with the payment side (decumulation). If a pension was just a savings plan, it would be much more straightforward. The payment part of a pension involves exchanging the bulk of these 'savings' into an income payable throughout retirement. It is the ratio between the amount being saved compared with the amount you would expect to receive in retirement that is the hardest to quantify.

With regards to the savings side, it is a matter of where the funds are invested and how the funds grow through to retirement. The Financial Services Authority (FSA) currently requires providers to quote (in most instances) 5%, 7% and 9% as assumed growth rates. These are not maximums or minimums. They are just examples. The actual growth rates will depend on where the funds are invested and how they actually perform.

Other factors to take into consideration are the charges associated with the scheme. The higher the charges, the less room there is for the fund to grow. Whilst the growth in funds can be hard to predict, the charges can be more easily determined.

Put in simplistic terms, the objective is to build up as higher fund value as possible for when you retire, ready to draw on those funds.

With regards to how much of a fund value you will require, the goal posts appear to continually move. It will be demonstrated later in this chapter how, for the retirement income required, a greater fund is now needed compared with previous years. The rise in funds needed (the decline in annuity rates) can be directly linked to people living longer. One of the main reasons why more funds are required is due to these funds having to last for a longer period of time.

The way I explain how a pension works is illustrated below:

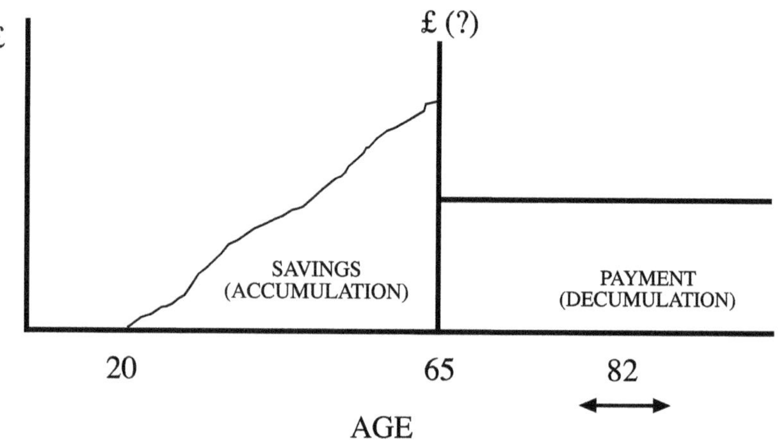

The above diagram partly demonstrates the need to start saving towards your retirement early. The earlier you start saving towards your retirement, the more money is saved and the longer the period you have to allow the funds to grow.

The diagram below demonstrates the effect of retiring early.

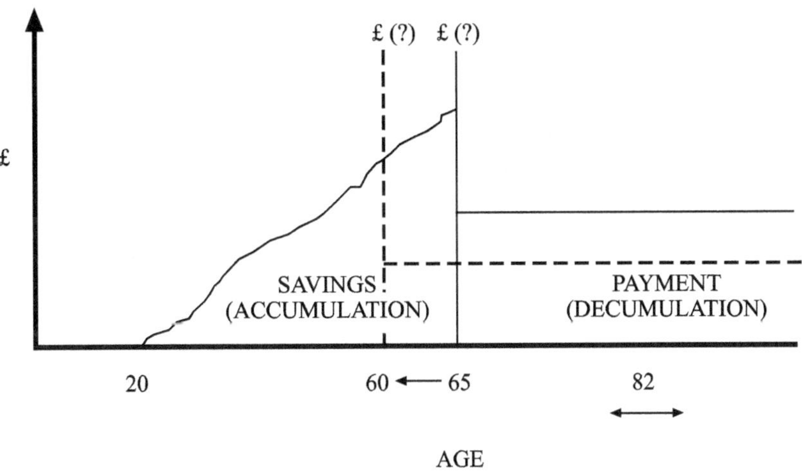

It can be very expensive to retire early. The reasons are threefold:

- Less time to save.
- Less time for the funds to grow.
- Longer period over which the pension is to be paid.

WHY DO YOU NEED TO SAVE MORE FOR YOUR RETIREMENT THAN BEFORE?

A typical view of life could be as follows:

Broadly speaking, you now have 2 working years for every 1 year in retirement. As discussed earlier, this ratio is likely to deteriorate as time in retirement lengthens.

Putting off saving towards your retirement could be very costly. By failing to make the most of your savings/working years, you are putting a sizeable dent in your potential retirement fund.

Another factor is the demise of the final salary/defined benefit pension scheme. Final salary schemes remain a feature of the public sector. There are pressures to review these terms in order to reduce the cost to the State. For private companies, there are comparatively very few schemes left. They have been replaced by defined contribution/money purchase pension schemes. There can be little doubt that final salary schemes have historically returned higher pension incomes than money purchase arrangements.

The third factor is the annuity rates that are offered. The table below demonstrates the reduction in rates in recent years. This corresponds with the improving longevity.

The table is based on a male, aged 65, single life, 5 years guarantee with payments remaining level.

The percentage figures below represents the income you can receive for the value of fund you have. For instance, an annuity rate of 10% means that for a fund value of £100,000, you would receive a guaranteed income for life of £10,000.

January 1991	15.20%	January 2002	8.11%
January 1992	13.68%	January 2003	7.08%
January 1993	12.45%	January 2004	7.34%
January 1994	10.41%	January 2005	7.17%
January 1995	11.63%	January 2006	6.88%
January 1996	10.92%	January 2007	7.10%
January 1997	10.90%	January 2008	7.32%
January 1998	10.05%	January 2009	7.22%
January 1999	8.75%	January 2010	6.76%
January 2000	9.11%	January 2011	6.40%
January 2001	9.05%	January 2012	5.80%

To summarise the effect of what this means, we will take the first of these years (1991) and the most recent (2012). In January 1991 when the annuity rate was 15.2%, you would have needed a fund of £131,579 to generate an income of £20,000 per annum. By January 2012, when the annuity rate had reduced to 5.8%, the fund you would have needed to generate the same level of income had risen to £344,828.

In 2012, you would need over double the fund to achieve the same income compared with 1991. Or, put it another way, you could have the same fund value in 1991 and 2012 but receive less than half the income in 2012 compared with if you had retired 21 years earlier.

During this period of time, annual pension statements could have revealed a rising pension fund but with little or no improvement in the projected income. Indeed, your pension fund could have risen but the projected income could easily have fallen taking into consideration the above deterioration in annuity rates.

For many savers I have spoken to, they look upon pensions as a waste of money. This is because it appears that no matter how much they contribute, their projected retirement income does not increase. This leads many to look at alternatives to pensions such as buy-to-let property or Individual Savings Accounts (ISAs). These types of arrangement are, however, less tax advantageous than pension plans. Whatever the investment, whether it is pensions, ISAs etc, the same principles still apply insofar that you still need an ever increasing retirement pot to last you for a longer period in retirement. Just because you can get at an ISA as a lump sum does not mean the same value will last you any longer than a pension.

HOW DO YOU SAVE FOR YOUR RETIREMENT?

Traditionally, retirement planning and pensions are synonymous with each other. This needn't be the case. As mentioned before, the objective is to gather a sum of money together to be used in retirement. This doesn't have to be from just one source.

The funds you require can be derived from a number of different sources including:

- Any savings/investments including ISAs
- Property
- Business assets
- Other assets that should rise in value such as fine wines, gold, stamps, paintings, vintage cars
- And/or any PENSION PLANS.

Pension plans/schemes carry a great deal of negative publicity in the media. There was the Daily Mirror pension scandal. This was where many lost the value of their pension plan due to their funds being effectively raided by certain individuals. Legislation was subsequently introduced to prevent such a recurrence in the future.

There are still occasions where members of pension schemes are reported to have lost all their funds. Some of these reported stories are often exaggerated. Nevertheless, any negative story regarding pensions, in general, can have the result that less people are likely to save via a pension in the future. This often also means that they may not have a plan to save towards their retirement, at all.

We all know of many people who have a comfortable retirement thanks to saving for much of their working lives in pension arrangements. And yet, good news stories regarding pensions are very rare.

If, for whatever reason, a pension plan is not the preferred way to save for retirement, discipline is needed to ensure that an alternative plan is put together. More importantly, it should be kept to.

ARE ISAs SUITABLE FOR RETIREMENT PLANNING?

The simple answer to this is – YES.
Are they 'better' than pensions? – SOMETIMES.

The first point that needs to be made is that pensions and ISAs can be invested in the same asset classes. You can have a cash ISA. You can also have a pension investing in cash/deposit funds. Similarly, ISAs can invest in shares/equities. So can pensions.

The main differences between the 2 involve the tax treatment and how you can draw the funds.

The best way to examine this is to look at the basic advantages and disadvantages they have over each other. Both ISAs and pensions are free of Capital Gains Tax. They are also both free of income tax apart from UK dividends. It is these tax breaks that make both ISAs and pensions suitable for retirement planning.

The main differences between the two are that pensions attract tax relief whereas ISAs don't. To demonstrate the effect of this, please see the example below:

Amount	Tax Relief	Total Invested
Pension	£100 + £25	= £125
ISA	£100 + £0	= £100

The advantages are clear to see. If we assume, say, a 5% annual growth, the effect is even more evident.

After one year, the ISA grows to £105 whereas the pension grows to £131.25. This extra £1.25 is as a result of the growth on the tax relief. This effect is referred to as *gross roll-up*. This effect is compounded the longer the funds are invested.

Whilst it is true that pensions are taxable in payment, you must take into account that ¼ / 25% of the fund can be taken as tax free cash. This means that ¾ / 75% of the fund is potentially taxable.

In order to examine the net effect of this, let us see the net result of the above:

	Amount	Tax Relief	Total Invested	Less tax deducted	TOTAL
Pens	£100	+£25	£125 + £6.25 = £131.25	£19.67	**£111.58**
ISA	£100	+£0	£100 + £5 = £105	£0	**£105.00**

On this basis, pensions give better returns compared with ISAs. This isn't, however, the whole picture.

ISAs have a major advantage insofar that you can take the whole fund as cash whenever you want. With pensions, only 25% of the fund is available as a tax free cash lump sum. The remainder of the fund is only usually available by way of a regular taxable income. In addition, you are prevented from drawing on your pension (in normal circumstances) prior to age 55. There is no such restriction with ISAs or, indeed, any other non pension investment.

WHEN SHOULD I START SAVING TOWARDS MY RETIREMENT?

Not only is it important to decide how to save for your retirement, the decision as to when to start saving is equally important.

The answer to this is quite simple – THE SOONER THE BETTER!

The same excuses that people use to put off other important decisions are used to delay contributing towards their retirement funds. For instance, there are the 'gunners'. They invariably say "I'm going to do this and I'm going to do that, just as soon as.....(please enter whatever excuse as appropriate)".

There are always pressures on an individual's finances – from buying a car and educational expenses when you are younger to buying a house/repaying the mortgage and raising a family, probably later in life. If you wait until the mortgage has been repaid and the children have 'flown the nest', you probably have not given yourself enough time to gather a big enough fund to be able to make the most of your retirement.

One of the issues is that when you are relatively young, retirement is a long way off. I agree that it starts out that way. Time does, however, have a nasty way of creeping up on you. In other words, time soon passes.

Another problem is that retirement is intangible. It is not a thing. It can mean different things to different people. A holiday or a new car is more tangible. They appear much more exciting to save towards rather than a pension. In many cases, people borrow to be able to buy the car or even the holiday. If this is the case, this means that there will inevitably be less money available to save towards retirement.

The trick is to try and enjoy life now but also put some money aside for the future as well.

THE STATE PENSION

The basic State Pension has fallen in value in real terms since its introduction in 1946. Despite this, the State Pension still forms the cornerstone of an individual's retirement planning for all but the wealthiest.

The main reason that the State Pension has, until recently, been falling in real terms is due to the value of the State Pension being raised by average prices (the Retail Price Index). This is opposed to being increased by National Average Earnings.

To demonstrate the trend in the UK basic State Pension, the table below shows the value of the State Pension as a percentage of average earnings:

1979 – 26%

1987 – 20%

2007 – 16%

(Source : National Statistics)

Recent steps have been taken in order to prevent this downward trend continuing. The Government has introduced legislation that means the State Pension will rise in real terms moving forwards.

To demonstrate the problem further;

- in 1941 there were 5.6 workers for each pensioner.
- in 2000, there were approximately 4 workers for each pensioner.

This ratio is set to get worse as people live longer.

This puts a huge burden on future taxpayers. This is because a much smaller number of taxpayers will have to fund a larger number of pensioners. In order to keep this public expenditure under control, legislation is already planned to increase the State Pension Age.

The State Pension age is set to rise for both men and women from age 65 to 68. This will be phased in between 2019 and 2046. Males born after the latter part of 1953 will be affected. For a more accurate age of when you can expect to draw the State Pension, please see http://pensions-service.direct.gov.uk/en/state-pension-age-calculator/home.asp

You may also obtain a State Pension forecast on line from www.thepensionservice.gov.uk

WHAT IS AN ANNUITY?

An annuity is historically the most common way to draw on your retirement fund. After any tax free cash is taken, the remainder of the fund is generally exchanged for a taxable income. This is traditionally by way of an annuity – an income for life.

You usually have several options when buying a traditional annuity. These options include the following:

■ A guarantee period of 5 or 10 years. You can nominate a **minimum period** of how long your pension is paid for irrespective of how long you live.

■ Whether a spouse's option is included. You can elect for all or a proportion of your pension to be payable to your spouse should you pre-decease them.

■ Escalation. You can elect for your income to increase by a fixed amount or in line with an index such as National Average Earnings (NAE) or Retail Price Index (RPI).

The inclusion of these options comes at a cost. The more options you select, the less income you will receive.

There may therefore be conflicting objectives. It may be important for you to ensure that an income is paid to your spouse after you die. On the other hand, you may need to maximise the income in order to maintain your standard of living. Choices need to be made and priorities established.

Many who come to draw on their benefits believe that the only options they have are the ones specified by their provider. This is frequently presented as 'tick box' options. There are usually many more options other than those presented by the provider. The Money Advice Service produces a free guide "Your Pension – It's time to choose". This goes some way to explain the options available.

The vast majority of the 'at retirement' market consists of those, coming up to retirement, exchanging their funds for a conventional or traditional annuity. If you have high blood pressure, high cholesterol, smoke, are overweight or have or have had a serious illness you could qualify for an impaired life or enhanced annuity. This would effectively increase the amount of income you would receive, often quite substantially. It has been estimated that up to 60% of those drawing their benefits would qualify for an impaired life/enhanced annuity.

Many mistakes are made as a result of not considering all the options available and not seeking to obtain the most favourable annuity rates available. It is for those reasons that this is one of those occasions where advice should ideally be sought.

ARE THERE ANY OTHER WAYS OF DRAWING MY RETIREMENT INCOME?

Not only have the options increased as to how to draw your benefits, they should be fully considered.

When the term 'annuity' is mentioned, this generally refers to a fixed income for the remainder of your life. A whole range of different annuities have been designed where the level of income is not necessarily fixed and can vary. With profits annuities and unit linked annuities are good examples of these.

Income drawdown is another option which has risen in popularity. Over the years, drawdown has been referred to as other things such as deferred annuity and unsecured income. More recently, this has been renamed as 'capped drawdown'. Another type of drawdown called 'flexible drawdown' has also been introduced.

Capped drawdown allows you to draw off the fund that has been accumulated for retirement. This is opposed to exchanging the whole fund for an income payable until death. Under this type of arrangement, the funds remain invested.

Flexible drawdown is only available if you have a secure pension income of at least £20,000 per annum. Providing this is in place, you have a great deal of flexibility in respect of how much and when you can draw from the fund.

Another alternative to a conventional/traditional annuity is what is referred to as a short term or fixed term annuity. These types of arrangement have grown in popularity and more providers have become involved in offering variations of these. This is where an income is received for a known period of time. At the end of this term, a maturity value is received. Unlike capped drawdown, there is no investment risk.

MAIN POINTS TO CONSIDER

✓ People are living longer and are spending a greater proportion of their life in retirement.

✓ It will cost you more to live in retirement than you think.

✓ The State Pension age is rising and will be at least 68 for those born after 1978.

✓ Saving for retirement can take on other methods of saving as well as, or in addition to, a pension plan.

✓ The same choice of investments is available to pensions as well as other investments including ISAs.

✓ The fund required to generate your desired income is likely to change.

✓ Review your plans regularly to ensure you remain on target to obtain the income you require for when you retire.

✓ At retirement, there are more options than you may be aware of and all options should be explored.

FINAL THOUGHTS

■ When would I like to retire - realistically?

■ How much am I expected to receive when I retire based on my current savings?

■ As a proportion of today's earnings, how much income will I need for when I retire?

■ Am I on target?

■ What charges are being paid in respect of my existing pension plans?

■ Where are my pension funds invested?

■ At retirement, what are my options and what is the maximum income I could obtain?

If you are not able to answer the above questions, you may need help or advice with regards to your financial planning needs.

CHAPTER 5

SAVINGS AND INVESTMENTS

- For what purpose are you investing?
- How long do you wish to invest for?
- What is your attitude to risk with regards to investing?

These are the three basic questions that need to be determined in deciding how you should invest or, indeed, whether you should be investing at all!

But before you even begin to think about whether to invest, aim to *repay or reduce your debt first.* This will include any overdraft, credit card debts, personal loans as well as your mortgage.

WHAT IS THE MAIN PURPOSE
FOR INVESTING?

The main aim in respect of investments is to put money aside for a time when it will or is likely to be needed. It is effectively storing income or capital for a future time when it is expected or more likely to be needed.

Investments can be used to provide a lump sum to help with retirement or to fund early retirement. The objective could be to invest for anything that requires a significant capital outlay. Typical examples could include a deposit for a house, car purchase or even a holiday of a lifetime.

Other common uses for investments involve the next generation. This could include:

- Funding for wedding expenses.
- Expenditure involved with further education.
- Helping with the deposit towards a property.
- To just give them 'a good start in life'.

The objective/purpose is the main factor to take into consideration. This will inevitably impact on the attitude to risk you are prepared to take as well as the likely timescales.

WHAT ARE YOUR TIMESCALES?

The requirement for funds within, say, 5 years would lead most financial advisers to look towards recommending more liquid assets. This would generally be bank deposits and should also include cash ISAs.

The longer the period above 5 years, the more appropriate it would be to consider other forms of investments.

Some investments would need to be for specific periods such as your selected retirement date or possible further education expenditure. Other costs such as wedding expenditure can be a little more difficult to time. The flexibility in terms of the length of investment period would therefore also need to be considered.

WHAT RISK ARE YOU PREPARED TO TAKE WITH REGARDS TO YOUR INVESTMENTS?

Assessing the attitude to risk is probably where most mistakes are made.

This topic is so important that it deserves a chapter to itself. Please therefore refer to Chapter 6 – Attitude to Risk.

At one end of the spectrum, you can have a client who keeps all their funds in cash or bank deposits. The other extreme is where a client invests in a relatively small number of shares or investment 'fads' such as technology funds. This can be often without knowing much about the investments. My experience is that the 'older' generation tends to hold most of their wealth in cash deposits.

It is unlikely that either of the above extremes will be appropriate to an individual's circumstances. This is why the attitude to investment risk is so important to enable the appropriate portfolio to be assembled.

A purely deposit based investment can easily be eroded by inflation over time. A purely share/equity based portfolio can be too volatile to be palatable for many. Cash is likely to feature in most cautious portfolios. Equally, shares may feature heavily in a more adventurous portfolio. Nevertheless, for a truly diversified investment strategy, other asset classes should also feature. This could include gilt edged Government securities (gilts), corporate bonds and property as well as international shares/equities.

IS TAXATION AN IMPORTANT FACTOR?

Whilst it is the purpose, the term and the risk factors that are the main ingredients in constructing a portfolio, the implications regarding tax also need to be taken into consideration. For instance, a high rate (40%) tax payer would have to pay an extra 20% tax on savings interest, income from a unit trust/OEIC and an investment bond.

Another consideration is that some investments will automatically attract an income tax charge of 20% irrespective of an individual's tax position. For a non–taxpayer, such investments should perhaps be avoided.

Any income that is earned is subject to Income Tax. Whilst income from investments is subject to income tax, investment gains are, in the main, subject to Capital Gains Tax (CGT). For a higher rate tax payer, a CGT rate of 28% is more favourable than an Income Tax charge of 40%. In addition, each of us has an annual CGT allowance which is seldom utilised. Based on the allowance for the tax year 2012/2013, this amounts to £10,600. With careful planning, any tax payable on investment gains can be minimised. This can be achieved by simply selecting the appropriate products (tax wrappers) in relation to the overall investment portfolio.

"The tax tail shouldn't wag the investment dog"

Tax is a very emotive subject. I am yet to meet anyone who likes paying tax. Whilst tax is an important consideration, it shouldn't be the **main** consideration.

An example here would be in respect of tax efficient plans including Enterprise Investment Schemes (EIS) and Venture Capital Trusts (VCTs). Both of these schemes have tax advantages. They are, however, also generally regarded as being relatively high risk. It would therefore be totally irresponsible for an adviser to recommend to a cautious client that they invest in either of these schemes just because of the tax breaks.

In order to reiterate, the main considerations where investments are concerned should be:

- Purpose.
- Timescales.
- Attitude to risk.

The tax position is a consideration (i.e. the tail) but not the main emphasis (i.e. the dog).

COMMON ERRORS WHEN IT COMES TO INVESTING

1. Failing to set investment objectives – how much do you need and when?

2. Investing without fully understanding.

3. Making investment decisions based on emotion – they should be based on analysis and common sense.

4. Attempting to try and predict the markets. History has shown us that this is difficult, if not impossible.

5. Get rich quick philosophies – the value of a portfolio in 6 months is less important if you plan to hold your investment for 5, 10 or even 20 years.

6. Avoid the 'herd' mentality – do not follow the crowd. Others may give the impression that they know what they are doing...but do they?

7. Unrealistic expectations - you cannot expect the highest rates of return from secure investments such as a deposit account.

8. Taking a profit too early or running a loss for too long – i.e. cashing in investments that have gained in value and hanging on to investments that have lost in the hope that the losses will be recouped.

9. Overlooking the time value of money – inflation will reduce the real value of money over time.

10. Investing without taking into consideration the effect on your tax situation.

ARE THERE ANY BENEFITS IN SAVING REGULARLY?

The simple answer to this is – *YES*. Rather than end this section here, I will try and expand. There are inevitably going to be falls as well as rises in most types of investments particularly where the stock market has an influence. Regular investing is a good way to smooth out the highs and lows of the stock market. This is often referred to as **pound-cost averaging.**

The main benefit of 'pound-cost averaging' is that it effectively reduces risk.

If you invest a lump sum, you face the risk of investing at the 'wrong time'. This could be just before a dramatic fall in the stock market. By investing monthly, you effectively iron out the peaks and the troughs. Please see the diagram below.

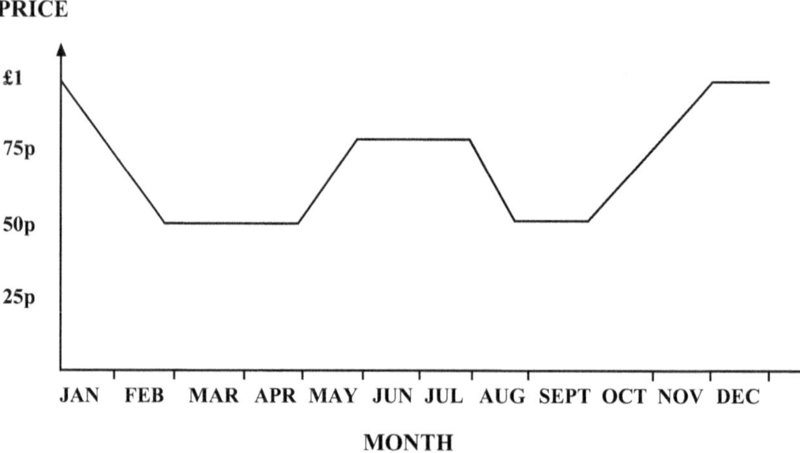

In order to emphasise the point, we will take the example of a £100 per month saving. Referring to the above diagram, the values of the investment are/were as follows:

MONTH	PRICE PER UNIT	MONTH	PRICE PER UNIT
January	£1	July	75 p
February	50 p	August	50 p
March	50 p	September	50 p
April	50 p	October	75 p
May	75 p	November	£1
June	75 p	December	£1

In other words, the value of the underlying holdings had not risen from the beginning of the year through to the end. The value of the investment was the same at the end of the year compared with the start of that year.

Let us, however, look at the effect of the price fluctuations throughout the year.

Month	Price	Units
January	£1	100
February	50p	200
March	50p	200
April	50p	200
May	75p	150
June	75p	150
July	75p	150
August	50p	200
September	50p	200
October	75p	150
November	£1	100
December	£1	100

The total of the units purchased during this year was 1,900. The total value at December was £1,900 (i.e. 1,900 units x £1 per unit). The total outlay was £1,200 over the year. This represents an investment gain of £700.

The reason why there is such a substantial gain is that during the year there were times when the price was low (i.e. 50p & 75p) compared with the final price of £1. Human nature tends to lead many people to selling their investments following a sharp fall. They fear that their investment may fall further. More experienced investors, however, may choose this opportunity to buy believing that prices were low and should therefore move upwards.

Although this may be considered an exaggerated demonstration of the possible positive effects of 'pound cost averaging', it is clear to see how investing monthly can be to your benefit.

It would be easy to see that if you were investing a lump sum, the best time to invest would have been in September. This means that you would have doubled your money in 2 months. However, you could have only have known this **after** the event.

In short, if you go on the basis that investments rise over a period of time, 'pound cost averaging' will have the effect of smoothing out any fluctuations you are likely to see.

SHOULD I JUST KEEP MY MONEY IN A BANK ACCOUNT?

Deposit accounts are a secure, safe and accessible place for your savings. They are also easy to understand. The returns are relatively predictable, particularly over the short term. The value of your fund does not fall. For your short terms needs, an immediate access deposit account is the ideal solution.

Deposit accounts are ideal for 'rainy day funds'. It is always a good idea to keep, say, 3 to 6 months' pay as an emergency fund. Should you keep any more funds than this on deposit? That depends on the individual. Those of you who are cautious in their outlook would probably want to have a larger emergency fund in order to cater for those unforeseen eventualities. Others have a more 'hand to mouth' financial existence and have no spare funds to save.

There are many reasons as to why keeping large sums on deposit is not necessarily a good idea:

Rates are at historically low levels

It is a struggle to find any accounts paying a good rate of interest. Many current accounts do not pay any interest at all.

Even if you discover an account that offers an attractive rate of interest to start with, this rate can soon fall later on. Introductory rates are usually high to start with but may go down over time.

Interest payable is taxable

The rate quoted is the gross rate payable. This is the rate before tax is deducted. For a basic rate taxpayer, 20% is deducted automatically. For a high rate taxpayer, 20% is deducted automatically with a further 20% payable.

To demonstrate what effect this has on returns, let us assume a 5% gross return. This rate makes it easier to demonstrate the basic maths involved:

- Non rate taxpayer = 5% return (providing they complete a R85 tax form)
- Basic rate taxpayer = 4% net return.
- High rate (40%) taxpayer = 3% net return.

Inflation can erode the spending power of your money

Many believe that by keeping your money on deposit is a way of ensuring that the value of your funds does not fall. This is not necessarily true. Tax and inflation both have the effect of reducing the real value of money. Let us assume a low inflation rate of 2% per annum. A basic rate taxpayer would need a gross interest rate 2.5% to counteract this. For a high rate taxpayer, the gross rate required is 3.333%. Any returns less than this and you are effectively losing money.

The effects of inflation should never be under-estimated. When people talk about risk with regards to money and investments, they immediately think of the risk of losing money. They may fear their investments falling in value. The risk associated with inflation can be just as damaging but in not so obvious a way.

It is for the above reasons that inflation is bad news especially for retired savers.

If you accept that not all your money should be kept on deposit, other asset classes should be considered.

You can usually get a better return elsewhere

It is a fact that shares/equities generally outperform cash over the medium to long term. There have been occasions when cash/deposits have outperformed shares. This is, however, the exception rather than the rule.

Some clients question this fact. I am not sure whether this is due to the media coverage of stock market investments or due to an investor's lack of tolerance with regards to losses.

Based on historic returns, shares have outperformed cash deposits 75% of the time where the investment period is a minimum of 5 years. This increases to 90% where the investment period is for a consecutive 10 years. (Source: Barclays Capital Equity Gilt study 2011).

Let's face it, any dramatic falls are emphasised in the media. When there was the BP oil spill in the Gulf of Mexico, it was mentioned what a detrimental effect that had on the price of their shares. The increase in the value of the company shares before or since has hardly been reported.

It is equally worth mentioning that we tend to remember losses more than we remember gains. There is also a tendency for some to believe that investing in shares can be akin to gambling.

SHOULD I INVEST IN AN ISA?

An Individual Savings Account (ISA) can mean different things to different people. When some people refer to an ISA, they automatically are referring to a cash ISA. For others, it is a stocks and shares ISA.

Many investments that are available via an ISA are readily available using other investments including a pension plan.

An ISA is a tax wrapper rather than a product. It is because of the tax advantages that ISAs offer that there are restrictions on how much can be invested in any one tax year.

The limits for the tax year 2012/2013 are as follows:

- Cash ISA - £5,640.
- Overall - £11,280

All of the overall amount can be invested in a stocks and shares ISA. This limit is reduced by half where an investor takes advantage of their cash ISA allowance.

The investments within an ISA are completely free of Capital Gains Tax (CGT). They are also free of income tax apart from on UK dividends that are paid with a notional 10% tax credit.

A cash ISA is, in effect, simply a deposit account without having to pay tax on the savings interest.

A stocks and shares ISA, on the other hand, is more of an investment. The underlying investment could be either:

- A unit trust
- An open ended investment company (OEIC)
- An investment trust.

For the purposes of this book, I will summarise the difference between each of the above rather than go into too much detail.

Unit trust

This is legally defined as a trust fund, managed for profit in accordance with a trust deed. These are open-ended funds. This means that these funds run indefinitely. More importantly, there is no minimum or maximum period of investment.

Open ended Investment company (OEIC)

This is a company which aims to make profits for its shareholders by dealing in securities, most commonly in other companies' shares. These are also open ended funds. There are many similarities between unit trusts and OEICs.

Investment trust

This is a company which aims to make profits for its shareholders by dealing in securities, most commonly in other companies' shares. Unlike unit trusts and OEICs, shares in investment trust companies are traded on the Stock Exchange. Investors can deal through a stockbroker, bank or via a financial adviser.

An investment ISA is therefore either a unit trust, OEIC or investment trust but with tax advantages.

Generally speaking, an ISA should be the first port of call with regards to investments and savings. This is whether you are investing a lump sum or regular monthly amounts. Only when your ISA allowance has been fully utilised should you look at other investments (tax wrappers) such as investment bonds or unit trusts/OEIC/investment trusts.

SHOULD I REVIEW MY INVESTMENTS?

As with most financial arrangements, regular reviews are important to ensure that you are on track to achieve your objectives. Please remember that if you are investing for the medium to long term, then short term fluctuations are not that significant. Day to day monitoring of your investments will do nothing but cause concern if there are sharp falls in the values. This is especially true if your attitude to risk is of a more cautious nature.

Knee jerk reactions to falls in the value of investments should be avoided. For instance, the tsunami in Japan had an adverse effect on the value of shares. I had a client contact me to ask if we should reduce their exposure to the Japanese sector. By the time the tsunami happened, it could be argued that it was too late. As it happened, the financial markets quickly recovered. To pull out of the Japanese market just after the tsunami would, with the benefit of hind-sight, been the wrong thing to do.

Although investments and the investment strategy should be reviewed periodically, these reviews should ideally not be used as an opportunity to change the portfolio just for the sake of it.

MAIN POINTS TO CONSIDER

✓ Inflation should be taken into consideration as it can eat into the value of your saving and investments.

✓ Over the medium to long term, it is a fact that keeping funds on deposit is unlikely to provide the greatest returns.

✓ Tax is an important factor but should not be the **main** factor when looking to invest.

✓ The main considerations for saving and investing are the purpose, timescales and the level of risk you are prepared to take.

✓ Avoid the common errors when it comes to investing.

✓ Review your plans regularly to ensure you remain on target to achieve your objectives.

FINAL THOUGHTS

■ What are my objectives with regards to my current savings/investments? What am I saving for?

■ Do I know where my funds are invested and what the risks are in respect of these funds?

■ Do I know what specific charges I am paying in relation to my savings/investments and what impact this has on my final return?

■ Are the timings of my investments aligned with the purpose of what they are invested for? [For example, there may be funds designated for retirement held in a bond maturing in 2 years, even though retirement may not be for another 20 years].

■ Are funds that I hold on deposit for any purpose other than for short-term objectives or to cover financial emergencies?

If you are not sure about the answers to any of the above questions, you may need help or advice in investigating matters further.

CHAPTER 6

FUND SELECTION

WHERE SHOULD I INVEST?

There is a vast array of different fund providers and different funds available.

These range from deposit accounts which are considered low risk as opposed to individual shares which are considered high risk. Please refer to the diagram below which represents, in general terms, the relationship between risk and reward.

Within each fund sector, there are also a number of different investment funds and 'star' investment managers. Anthony Bolton at Fidelity gained a good reputation for outperforming its sector with the Fidelity Special Situations fund which he managed for a number of years.

Rating agencies such as Morningstar try to assist in the selection of funds by categorising funds and their managers.

I am often asked questions such as:

"Do you think gold is a good investment?"

"Should I invest in China?"

"Do you think Neil Woodford will perform well as a fund manager?"

"Is now a good time to invest in the stock-market?"

The truthful answer to all these questions (and many others) is -

I DON'T KNOW.

Unfortunately, this isn't what people want to hear. They would prefer certainty not uncertainty. We all would prefer a definitive answer to whatever question it is we are asking.

The competence of a professional is often gauged by their knowledge of the subject. If a doctor or car mechanic consistently said that they could not diagnose what was wrong with you or your vehicle, you'd probably think they weren't very good. Fund selection is however based on the past being the benchmark for the future. Whilst a significant fall in the markets should eventually lead to a subsequent rise, no one can definitely say this will happen or, indeed, when.

Some advisers try to play 'Mystic Meg' and predict the future. I think that, in many situations, this is doing their clients a great disservice. The more vague their prediction – the more accurate they are likely to be correct. For instance, if you predicted that the FTSE 100 will rise in the coming year, there is a 50% chance you will be correct. And more importantly, nobody will know whether the prediction was right or not until **after** the event.

This point is covered well in a very good book entitled "Fooled by Randomness" written by Nassim Nicholas Taleb.

At this point, you may be thinking - what value has a financial adviser in the fund selection process?

When concentrating solely on fund selection, I firmly believe that a good financial adviser's duty is firstly to establish a client's attitude to investment risk. Based on these findings, the next step is then to construct a diversified portfolio in keeping with the client's attitude to risk. It is the duty of the adviser to explain the rationale behind the portfolio. The final part is then to review the portfolio as well as the client's circumstances to ensure the plans, that are put in place, remain on track.

In order to summarise, the steps are:

1. Assess attitude to risk.
2. Construct a diversified portfolio utilising a number
    of different funds.
3. Review the portfolio regularly.

Of course, you may believe (with or without justification) that you can do better yourself. If you firmly believe this, you may choose to live without an adviser. This scenario is the whole point of this book. For some, an adviser is needed. For others, they are an unnecessary part of the process.

WHAT IS THE MOST IMPORTANT FACTOR TO TAKE INTO ACCOUNT WHEN INVESTING?

Research has shown that the most important factor with investing is ***asset allocation***. According to the Brinson study published in the Financial Analysts Journal in the early 1990's, as much as 91% of the variability of a portfolio's return may be attributed to its asset allocation.

The diagram below illustrates this

Asset Allocation.....

.......is the key driver of long term investment returns

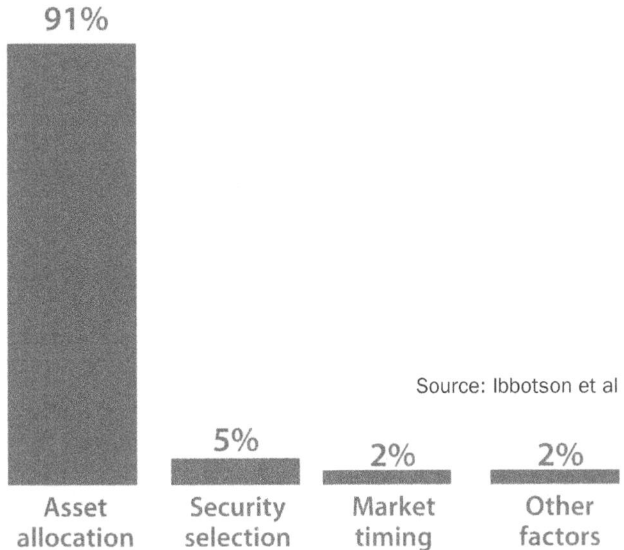

You will see from the above diagram that **2% is attributed to market timing**. Many I have spoken to would believe that this figure should be much higher. I accept that for those who have insider knowledge, timing can have more of an influence. For the rest of us, I would agree that the 2% figure is accurate.

It must be stressed at this point that insider dealing is illegal!

Amongst the financial services fraternity, the phrase that is used is that "It is the time in the market" that is the most important factor. This is because there have been certain days/times when there have been significant rises in the price of shares. To miss out on these days would be to the detriment of the overall performance.

The diagram below illustrates the effect of investing on the best and worst days over the last 20 years.

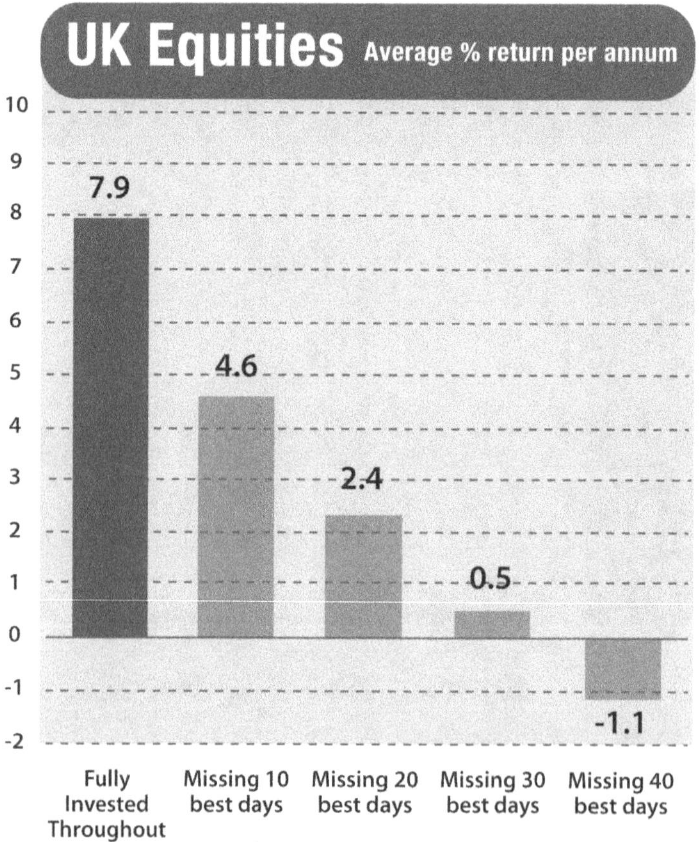

Source: FTSE All-Share Index average returns, Datastream and M&G Statistic, income reinvested as at 31.10.11

Security selection accounts for 5%. Again, many I have spoken to are surprised by this figure. Their belief is that this figure should be much higher. I would counter this by saying "why don't experts such as Warren Buffet just own one stock?" I was once informed that Warren Buffet owned 300 out of the 400 available stocks in a particular index. That sounds very much like diversification to me and definitely NOT stock picking.

Fund managers need to show us that there is some value in the extra layer of charges that their involvement demands. This is why many of the fund houses have a marketing budget to get this fact across.

The reality is that research has shown that over a 5 year period, 76% of all fund managers fail to outperform the market. This figure rises to 87% over a 10 year period. These figures don't even take into account those funds that have failed early on and cannot even establish a 5 or 10 year record.

The diagram below gives the percentages for when a fund manager has failed to outperform 'the market'

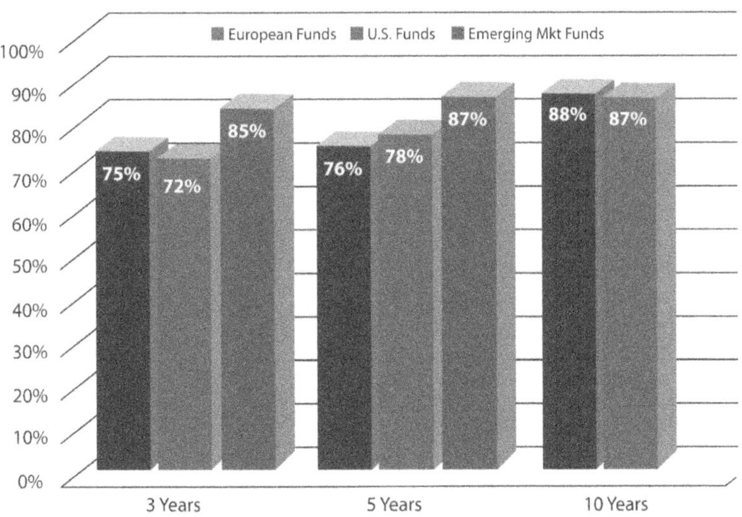

Source: Lipper, MSCI, S&P, Vanguard

WHAT IS ASSET ALLOCATION?

This takes into account the different areas or asset classes where you can invest. It is then a matter of constructing a portfolio by selecting a proportion or percentage of each of those assets. Once the assets are allocated, the individual holdings are then selected.

Examples of the most commonly used asset classes include:

- UK equities (shares).
- Overseas/international equities (shares).
- UK bonds/gilts.
- Corporate bonds.
- Overseas government bonds.
- Cash.
- Commercial property.

This can be widened further to include:

- Index linked securities.
- Commodities including gold.
- Hedge funds.

The idea is that a portfolio would consist of a wide variety of different funds within different sectors. This reduces risk.

The diagram below shows how an asset class may perform well in one year but not so well the next year.

Year							
2001	Japan -26.7%	Europe -20.9%	UK -13.6%	North America -12.5%	Emerging Markets -2.5%	Asia Pacific -2.0%	Corporate Bonds 4.7%
2002	North America -32.7%	Europe -25.8%	UK -23.0%	Japan -18.2%	Asia Pacific -17.4%	Emerging Markets -14.2%	Corporate Bonds 6.5%
2003	Corporate Bonds 5.3%	North America 14.3%	UK 22.3%	Japan 23.3%	Europe -26.9%	Asia Pacific 34.1%	Emerging Markets 41.0%
2004	North America 1.2%	Corporate Bonds 5.4%	Japan 6.1%	Asia Pacific 8.6%	UK 12.5%	Europe 13.5%	Emerging Markets 15.8%
2005	Corporate Bonds 6.8%	North America 18.5%	UK 20.7%	Europe 24.9%	Asia Pacific 32.3%	Japan 43.5%	Emerging Markets 50.7%
2006	Japan -14.5%	North America -1.4%	Corporate Bonds -0.7%	UK 17.2%	Emerging Markets 17.3%	Asia Pacific 17.7%	Europe 18.5%
2007	Japan -11.0%	Corporate Bonds -0.7%	UK 1.8%	North America 4.5%	Europe 12.6%	Emerging Markets 34.8%	Asia Pacific 36.4%
2008	Emerging Markets -37.0%	Asia Pacific -33.2%	UK -32.3%	Europe -24.6%	North America -18.5%	Corporate Bonds -10.3%	Japan -2.6%
2009	Japan -3.4%	Corporate Bonds 14.3%	North America 19.1%	Europe 19.4%	UK 30.4%	Asia Pacific 52.4%	Emerging Markets 57.7%
2010	Corporate Bonds 6.8%	Europe 8.3%	UK 17.3%	North America 17.7%	Japan 19.1%	Asia Pacific 21.3%	Emerging Markets 22.7%

You will see that Asia Pacific rose 36.4% during 2007. The following year (2008), it fell by 33.2%. One year, it was the top performing asset class – the next year it was one of the worst. Whilst this is an extreme example, this is often true of other asset classes.

Take property, for example. UK property rose in value consistently from 1996 through to 2006. I know of people who believed that property could do nothing but rise. That was until 2007 when we started to see a fall.

An analogy I was given in order to illustrate the value of a diversified portfolio was that "rather than bet on one horse, you bet on the whole race". Remember, if you bet on just one horse, that is gambling.

IS ASSET ALLOCATION REALLY THAT IMPORTANT?

The short answer to this is …YES. I have seen portfolios that have been invested 100% in property. Some portfolios have all their available funds invested in a technology fund from the days when that sector became 'in vogue'.

More recently, there has been a focus on the BRIC (Brazil, Russia, India and China) economies as well as gold.

The idea is that if you invest in these areas, you will get a higher return than if you invested in more traditional ways. In effect, you would be taking more of a punt on a particular sector than you would under normal asset allocation rules.

If you wish to take more of a gamble on certain geographical areas or individual shares then that is up to you. After all, it is your money. But that is not what I would term as investing. It is certainly not taking into account the attitude to risk that you would normally wish to take.

If you are saving towards your retirement, for example, you would not ideally wish to 'gamble' with your retirement fund. After all, your financial welfare in retirement will depend on it.

HOW CAN DIVERSIFICATION BE ACHIEVED?

Investing in just two shares can offer some diversification and thus reduce risk.

We could put all our savings in to one particular holding. I would class this move as more speculative than investing. This could ultimately be a very wise move. Equally, this could be a bad move if that share performed particularly badly. By diversifying between 2 shares, you reduce the risk of one performing particularly badly. This diversification can be extended further so that you are not reliant on one particular share, sector or even asset class. That is the whole purpose of diversification.

There are a number of organisations that employ, what are referred to, as *stochastic modelling* techniques. These techniques are generally based on past financial data as giving an insight into the future. After all, we can't predict the future and so historic data is all we have to go on.

Past returns cannot offer an exact guide to the levels of future returns from any investment or combination of investments. The past returns seen on any asset class or individual investment reflect the unique circumstances of the time, which will never be the same again. It is for these very reasons that past performance can only be used as a *guide* to future returns.

By this time we would have already established the attitude to risk. This would be one of the key components in putting together a portfolio.

An example of a portfolio for a medium/moderate risk investor would be as follows:

- Cash – 5%
- Fixed interest – 30%
- Property – 10%
- UK equity – 35%
- Overseas equity – 20%.

This gives a rough outline of what asset classes should be considered and what proportion should be given to each sector. It is then a matter of breaking this down further.

If we consider the sector of UK shares, we may need to consider small as well as large UK companies. For international shares, we may want to look at the geographical split as well as the size of the companies.

IS THERE A MORE SIMPLE WAY OF ACHIEVING DIVERSIFICATION?

An alternative way of diversifying without picking individual funds would be to look towards a packaged solution. Many fund managers offer a fund of funds solution or a suite of managed funds. Balanced managed, cautious and defensive managed funds are commonplace. Their objective is to manage the fund on your behalf. Although these funds give the appearance of being just one fund, the diversification is achieved 'behind the scenes'.

Providing the fund or combination of funds match the attitude to risk, this can be a simpler straightforward way of achieving the diversification that is recommended without 'over-egging' the detail.

In effect, this method of diversification involves buying into a readymade solution involving one or possibly more existing established funds. Another method is to have someone put together a bespoke portfolio. For instance, a stockbroker or discretionary fund manager may be utilised. Using a stockbroker or fund manager with discretionary powers can be a viable option. This is more commonly used for larger portfolios of, say, over £100,000/£150,000.

This is very similar in some ways to investing in a fund of funds or managed solution. The main difference is that a stockbroker/fund manager has the expertise to invest in individual shares. The argument is that they can put together a personalised/bespoke portfolio that can be comprised of individual funds and/or other funds, as I have covered already.

More recently, there has been a trend towards risk based portfolios. This could be viewed as a half way house between a fund of funds and a discretionary managed fund. The provider will typically establish a suite of different portfolios. These could be based on an individual's attitude to risk. Model portfolios will then be used that are appropriate to the circumstances. For instance, a client may have a cautious attitude to risk and is looking for capital growth. A 'ready-made' portfolio of different funds would then be selected. This portfolio would be amended depending on the performance of the funds within the portfolio. The portfolio would also be re-balanced regularly to ensure the risk associated with the portfolio was maintained.

WHAT IS RE-BALANCING?

Re-balancing is a process that should be adopted to ensure the selected portfolio maintains the level of risk that was selected from the outset. To demonstrate this, let us take the following as a sample portfolio:

- UK equities – £100,000 (50%).
- Fixed interest – £50,000 (25%).
- Cash – £50,000 (25%).

Using this example - if during the year, equities rose by 10%, cash stayed the same and fixed interest fell by 10%, the portfolio would now look like this:

- UK equities – £110,000 (54%).
- Fixed interest – £45,000 (22%).
- Cash – £50,000 (24%).

Although there was no material change in the composition of the portfolio, the weighting has changed due to the assets classes performing differently.

On the basis that the client's risk profile had not changed, it would be appropriate to re-balance the portfolio by 'selling' the 4% UK equities and buying more fixed interest and cash in order to get the portfolio proportionately back to where it was.

There are often debates as to how often re-balancing should occur. For individual portfolios or ready-made portfolios, this should be dealt with regularly – at least annually. This could be manually dealt with by the adviser or part of an automated process. With 'ready-made' funds such as managed or fund of funds, it is the manager that removes the need to re-balance as this is dealt with as part of their duties.

IS TIME A CONSIDERATION WITH REGARDS TO SELECTING FUNDS?

Attitude to risk is a major factor in choosing the most appropriate asset classes. The length of time for the investment process should also be considered. The more volatile the fund, the more likelihood there is of suffering a loss over the short to medium term. As time progresses, the effect of volatility is lessened.

For investment periods of less than 5 years, it is difficult to recommend funds other than those with low volatility such as cash. As a rule, the shorter the period of investment, the lower the risk the portfolio should be. Some risk profile questionnaires reflect the importance of time with regards to investment selection. The shorter the period of time for investment will result in a leaning towards a lower risk than would have otherwise been the case.

HOW DO I OBTAIN INFORMATION REGARDING FUNDS?

If we are going on the basis that you do not wish to use a financial adviser, there is a vast array of sources to choose from. Examples of reputable websites that financial advisers themselves use are as follows:

Morningstar
www.morningstar.co.uk – analyses and researches funds.

Trustnet
www.trustnet.com – fund research database.

Financial Express
http://webfund5.financialexpress.net/broadsheet/broadsheet.wsp.

SHOULD I REVIEW THE FUNDS THAT I INVEST IN?

It is always a good idea to review your plans regularly. With regards to the specific fund selection, there may be less of a need to amend the fund choice especially if the original asset allocation was arranged correctly.

Moving funds may involve further costs. Be wary of situations where you are advised to continually move funds or providers.

As mentioned before, it is the asset allocation that is the main emphasis rather than the individual funds. Providing the asset allocation remains in accordance with your attitude to investment risk, the need to amend funds should be considered but not necessarily acted upon. That being said, there is little point in sticking with a fund that consistently performs below its particular benchmark.

MAIN POINTS TO CONSIDER

✓ It is the asset allocation that is the most important factor rather than market timing or fund selection.

✓ It is very difficult to time the market.

✓ Predicting the future is impossible for most mortals.

✓ Even widely acclaimed fund managers hold a wide range of holdings rather than select/pick a few securities.

✓ Some fund managers out-perform the markets. Many do not.

✓ There is less chance of a risk of loss the longer a fund is held. This is especially true of more volatile funds.

✓ Diversification can be achieved and maintained by using managed funds, fund of funds or other 'packaged solutions'.

✓ Your fund selection should be reviewed regularly as things will inevitably change.

FINAL THOUGHTS

- Do I know what funds I am invested in?

- Am I invested in more than one fund with one company?

- Am I invested in individual funds or is there a process for managing my funds?

- Are my funds re-balanced on a regular basis?

If you are not sure about the answers to any of the above questions, you may need help or advice in investigating matters further.

CHAPTER 7

ATTITUDE TO RISK

When advising on investments, there are 3 main questions that I need to ask:

1. What are you saving for / what is the purpose?
2. How much do you intend to save or invest?
3. How long do you intend to save/invest for?

Apart from these questions the only other thing you need to ascertain is – what is your attitude to investment risk?

It is also worth pointing out that the purpose, amount and period of investment also has an impact on the attitude to risk.

WHAT IS MEANT BY ATTITUDE TO RISK?

This can be very subjective because high risk for one person can be interpreted as medium risk for another. In addition, a person's attitude to risk can change due to their experiences.

As a general rule, no-one should ever invest in anything that will cause them to lose sleep at night. Nevertheless, being ultra cautious could also mean that you potentially lose out over a period of time. This would not only be due to the effect of inflation but also due to the historic higher returns that other asset backed investments usually provide.

We all want a 20% return (or even more) from a rock solid deposit account. Unfortunately, this isn't how investing works. Generally speaking - the higher the risk, the higher the return.

WHAT FACTORS DETERMINE ATTITUDE TO RISK?

Although attitude to risk is important in itself, other factors can determine the risk you would wish to take. For instance:

Purpose – you may be prepared to take a greater risk for investments/savings towards plans that take lesser importance to you than those that you make a priority to achieve. For example, when investing a lump sum to provided for your children's education, I would usually expect to see a more cautious approach.

Period – the longer you have to invest, the higher the risk you might want to take. This is because there would be more time to correct any losses that occur during adverse economic cycles.

Amount – there is a big difference to saving £50 per month compared with investing £100,000 as a lump sum. I would suggest that there is much more likely to be a cavalier attitude to the former rather than the latter. This would be reflected in the risk that you would be prepared to take.

Another consideration that is worthy of mention is related to the period of time that you are prepared to invest for: **AGE**.

As a general rule, the older you are the more cautious you are in your outlook. It could be that your greatest earning potential period is behind you. You would therefore wish to preserve your capital rather than risk a significant proportion of it.

Most pension arrangements now have lifestyling facilities to cater for the fact that we tend to be more cautious as we draw nearer to retirement.

WHAT IS LIFESTYLING?

Lifestyling is an investment strategy that is becoming more commonly used with pension plans. It allows you to benefit from potentially higher returns during the earlier years of saving, while increasing the safety of the fund in the years immediately before retirement.

Lifestyling could easily be placed in the Chapters concerning retirement planning, investments or even fund selection. The reason why it is synonymous with retirement planning is because it is usually associated with pension investments. The reason why it could be in the investments section is because it is more of an investment strategy. And finally, the reason it could be associated with fund selection is because it usually involves switching funds as retirement draws nearer.

I have nevertheless chosen to include lifestyling in the risk profile section as it demonstrates how you should consider switching to more cautious funds as you draw closer to retirement (i.e. as the term of investment shortens).

The objective is to maximise growth in the earlier years of saving whilst switching to safer investments in order to avoid catastrophic falls in the market just prior to retirement.

The initial investments are determined by the attitude to risk you wish to take.

Contributions can be invested in shares or other assets in keeping with your attitude to investment risk. Gradually, usually within 5 - 10 years of retirement, the investment is switched to more secure funds including bank deposits and gilt edged securities (gilts). This can be done gradually or on fixed pre-determined milestones (e.g. your birthday).

As retirement approaches, the fund should be invested almost entirely in low risk/secure funds. Of course, this strategy would not work nearly as well for those wishing to adopt a low risk/cautious investment strategy to start with.

Although this strategy is designed to safeguard funds nearer retirement, there can be situations where you can miss out. This is where funds are switched to bank deposits/gilts just prior to a sudden increase in the returns from other asset backed investments such as the stock market.

HOW DO YOU DETERMINE ATTITUDE TO RISK?

There are a number of ways this can be achieved. These days, many advisers use a risk profiling process to help determine a client's attitude to investment risk.

It is always helpful to see what type of risk a client has taken in the past. This is by no means a firm indication of what risk they are likely to want in the future. Instances of this are where they have been sold a fund that is not appropriate for them. Another example is where a fund or even an individual share has been purchased for more emotive reasons. In any case, attitudes to investment risk do change and there is a tendency for us all to become more cautious in our outlook.

Care must be taken where a client believes they are, for example, medium risk. Clarification as to what they mean needs to be established. One person's idea of medium risk could be different from that of someone else. Indeed, an adviser could have a different viewpoint. This is why a risk profiling process needs to be adopted. If for no other reason, this may just confirm what is already known.

These days, the main method of clarifying risk is by use of a questionnaire. This would usually be multiple choice where one of several answers would be selected.

There are a number of questionnaires out there. Some are better than others. I have seen one questionnaire with as few as 3 questions! It is my belief that this is far too few questions to be able to gather anything other than a general view. The more questions there are the more accurate the results are likely to be.

I have included one such attitude to risk questionnaire for you to complete yourself. You will be able to use the table to mark yourself and assess your own attitude to investment risk.

RISK PROFILE QUESTIONNAIRE

Please select the answer that most accurately reflects your views.

Time horizon
____

When do you expect to begin taking withdrawal(s) from your investment?

A. In less than 4 years

B. In 5-7 years

C. In 8-10 years

D. In 11 years or never expect to take withdrawals

Attitude to investment risk

Question 1

Inflation can erode the return on your portfolio. For example, in a typical year with a 3.5% inflation rate, a portfolio with a 6% return before inflation would have a real return of only 2.5% (6% - 3.5% = 2.5%). However, investments that are expected to beat inflation over time may experience short-term losses.

Which of the following statements best reflects your views toward investment risk and the effects of inflation?

A   My main aim is to avoid loss even if I may earn less than the rate of inflation..0

B   While I will accept a low level of volatility, my main goal is to earn slightly more than inflation... 4

C   I am willing to accept some volatility for a chance to increase the value of my portfolio and outperform inflation over time..10

D   I am willing to accept higher volatility for a chance to maximise the return of my portfolio and to outperform inflation...........17

Points___________

Question 2

Let us presume you invested £20,000 in an investment account this year with the intention of holding it for ten years. If this investment were to lose value during the first year, at what value of your initial £20,000 investment would you move to a more conservative option?

A. £19,000 (Loss 5%)..0

B. £18,000 (Loss 10%)..4

C. £17,000 (Loss 15%)..8

D. £16,000 or less (Loss 20% or more)............................. 12

E. I would not move to a more conservative option...................17

Points___________

Question 3

**The following table shows the probable performance of four hypothetical portfolios over a 20 year holding period.
In which of the following portfolios would you prefer to invest?**

	Possible number of years with negative	Possible worst 1 yea annual return	Possible 20 year average annual return
Portfolio 1	3	-7%	5.3%
Portfolio 2	5	-22%	6.3%
Portfolio 3	6	-26%	7.8%
Portfolio 4	7	-33%	8.2%

A. Portfolio 1...0

B. Portfolio 2...6

C. Portfolio 3..10

D. Portfolio 4..17

Points___________

Question 4

The following graph shows a hypothetical one year return on £25,000 invested in five portfolios. The best potential and worst potential returns are presented.

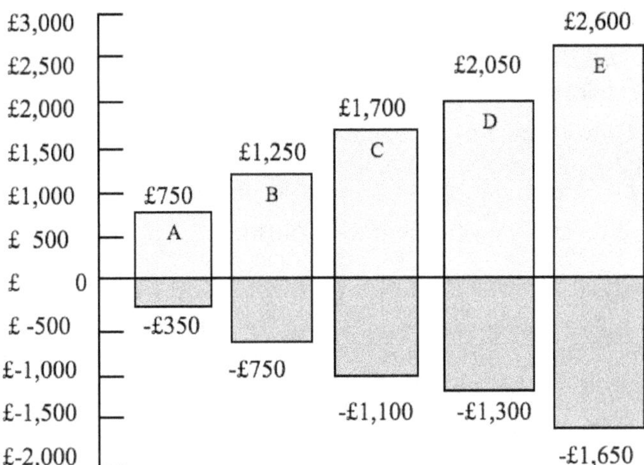

A. Portfolio A 0
B. Portfolio B 4
C. Portfolio C 8
D. Portfolio D 12
E. Portfolio E 17

Points__________

Question 5

The following statements describe the most likely gain, as well as the chance of loss, on £100,000 invested for one year in five hypothetical portfolios. Which portfolio would you select?

A. Most likely gain at the end of one year is £5,500.
   However, there is an 18% chance of a negative return............0

B. Most likely gain at the end of one year is £6,800. However,
   there is a 24% chance of a negative return...........................4

C. Most likely gain at the end of one year is £8,300. However,
   there is a 30% chance of a negative return...........................9

D. Most likely gain at the end of one year is £9,200. However,
   there is a 33% chance of a negative return...........................12

E. Most likely gain at the end of one year is £10,400. However,
   there is a 44% chance of a negative return...........................17

Points__________

Question 6

Investing involves a trade-off between risk and returns, as depicted in the diagram below. Three portfolios are shown in this diagram in order of increasing risk and return. Which of the following portfolios would you choose?

Conservative investments   Risky investments
Lower risk   Higher risk
Lower expected returns   Higher expected returns

Portfolio 1   Portfolio 2   Portfolio 3

A. Portfolio 1 – I am most concerned with limiting my risk and I
   am willing to accept low to moderate growth potential...........0

B. Portfolio 2 – I am willing to accept a moderate level of risk and possible short-term downturns in order to seek medium to high growth potential...7

C. Portfolio 3 – I am willing to accept a high level of risk and a possibility of longer downturns in order to seek maximum growth potential...15

Points___________

Risk tolerance score

Total score ____

(Risk tolerance score = sum of points from question 1 through to question 6).

Selecting a portfolio

The summary scoring grid below supports the final portfolio recommendation process by combining the time horizon and risk tolerance scores. To use the scoring grid, find the time horizon score on the horizontal axis and the risk tolerance score on the vertical axis. The intersection of these two points is the recommended portfolio.

Summary scoring grid

	Time horizon choice			
Risk tolerance score	A	B	C	D
0 – 11	N/A	Low	Low	Low
12 – 33	N/A	Low to medium	Low to medium	Low to medium
34 – 55	N/A	Medium	Medium	Medium
56 – 84	N/A	Medium	Medium to high	Medium to high
85 – 100	N/A	Medium	Medium to high	High

You will see from the above that it is hard to justify any investments for a period of less than 4 years in anything other than low risk investments.

I must emphasise that this is just one of many questionnaires out there. In addition, it is not normally good form to include a system whereby you can mark the answers yourself as it is believed that this can influence the outcome. For the purposes of this book, this is included just as an example as part of the process for establishing attitude to risk.

These questionnaires are by no means foolproof. They do, however, provide a more objective assessment than the subjective views of the adviser or the client.

The Financial Services Authority (FSA) produced a bulletin in January 2011 on the subject of risk entitled "Proposed guidance on Assessing Suitability: Establishing the risk a customer is willing and able to take and making a suitable investment selection". This makes reference to the fact that some risk profiling processes were not as robust as they should be.

The FSA made specific mention that advisers should make plans for clients based on three main factors:

- Risk tolerance.
- Risk capacity.
- Their goals.

Risk capacity was highlighted as an important factor that advisers often failed to take into consideration. For instance, you are more likely to be averse to risk if the £50,000 that was being invested was the only money you had left. This would, however, not be such as big a deal for someone who had a further £1 million invested elsewhere.

CAN YOU AVOID RISK?

The answer to this is straightforward – NO.

Some of you may think of risk as being a fall in the capital value. This risk is associated with most types of investing. This is referred to as *capital risk.* The main conventional way of avoiding this type of risk is by using bank or building society deposits whether they are for a fixed term period or not.

Other risks include:

- Inflation risk.
- Shortfall risk.
- Interest rate risk.
- Currency risk.

Bank or building society deposit accounts offer relative security with little risk to the capital value. The main risk here is with regards to inflation. Inflation can reduce the real value of the monies deposited. Where inflation is higher than the rate of interest paid, as seen in recent years, you are effectively losing money. The true value of your capital is certainly not being protected for the future.

Another risk associated with a deposit account investment is interest rate risk. If you fix the rate of interest in a bond for 2, 3, 4 or even 5 years, you would hope that the interest rates go down over that period or at least stay the same. Otherwise, you risk locking into a rate that would end up being non-competitive. The reverse can happen with fixed interest mortgages.

Shortfall risk is another risk worth mentioning. For example, you may be saving towards your retirement. If you are targeting a specific amount in order to maintain your standard of living in retirement, you will want your money to work for you. If you use deposit funds or money market funds, you risk there being a shortfall in the target income you require.

Currency risk only applies where investments (including deposits) are denominated in a different currency from the pound. It is very rare that the pound will remain at the same exchange rate compared with other major currencies such as the Euro or the US dollar. If your investments are denominated in these or other currencies, this adds extra risk.

There are some relatively low risk investments that are worthy of special mention. Although they could be considered low risk, they are not totally without risk.

Some ***products that offer capital guarantees or are capital protected*** can also carry some level of risk. Again, inflation can reduce the value of the investment in real terms. A further risk associated with these types of plans is in connection with the strength of the guarantee or protection. Who is it that is providing the guarantee? Can they keep their promise? The underlying structure of some of these investments may mean they are considered more higher than lower risk even though the terms 'guaranteed' or 'capital protected' are used.

Index linked savings (e.g. Index Linked National Savings Certificates or index linked gilt edged securities) offer some protection against inflation. Many of these types of investments are issued for a fixed period of time. Rather than invest in an individual holding, there are funds that invest in a basket of different holdings. The capital value of these funds can fall as well as rise. This is because the price of the investments can vary depending on demand and supply. If you therefore wanted to surrender your investment, you would receive the value at that point in time. Although these types of investment offer protection against inflation, the capital value can fall. It is for these reasons that these types of investment are not considered as safe (or low risk) as deposit accounts. Although these plans are intended to guard against inflation risk, there remains some exposure to capital risk, shortfall risk and interest rate risk.

Gilt edged securities (gilts) are issued by the Government as a way of the Government borrowing from individuals, companies and institutions. The certificates used to be edged in gold which is how they get their name. This also signifies how safe they are. The UK Government has never defaulted on its debt. If you therefore buy a single gilt and hold it through to when it matures, you are 'guaranteed' to receive a pre-determined rate of interest plus a 'guaranteed' capital amount back on the maturity date.

The main risk associated with this type of investment is interest rate risk. By locking into a 'guaranteed' rate, this rate won't look as attractive if interest rates rise. Capital risk also applies. The value of the investment is subject to market forces if the assets are traded before they mature. This can result in losses or gains. These funds are also subject to inflation risk and shortfall risk as with the other low risk investments mentioned earlier.

As mentioned in previous chapters, it is better to diversify where possible. A blend of index linked funds, fixed interest funds (including gilts) and bank/building society deposits could be more suitable for a low risk investor rather than concentrating on just one asset class (normally cash).

IS YOUR ATTITUDE TO RISK LIKELY TO CHANGE?

YES. As with most things in life, nothing stays constant.

It has been mentioned earlier that the older you get the more cautious you become...generally speaking. It is for these reasons that your attitude to risk should be periodically re-assessed.

Other life events may also have an impact. An inheritance or lottery win could lead to a more cavalier attitude to risk. On the other hand, a financial setback such as the loss of a job may result in a much more cautious view on risk.

It is worth mentioning that you may have differing attitudes towards risk depending on what you are saving for. Let us look at three possible reasons for saving/investing as follows:

- Retirement.
- Children's university fees.
- A deposit for a house.

You may, for example, have a medium attitude to risk/risk grade 5 out of 10. This may not tell the whole story. It is not unreasonable for you to want lower risk investments when saving for children's university fees compared with your retirement planning. What I am trying to point out is that there can be different attitudes to risk for each objective you have despite the overall investment risk attitude. Whether there should be a separate risk profile assessment for each objective is open to discussion. I, personally, believe that that is taking things too far. Either way, differing objectives needs to be taken into consideration.

DOES THE RISK PROFILING PROCESS DETERMINE YOUR ATTITUDE TO INVESTMENT RISK?

Ultimately, it is you who should decide what risks you would wish to take. The role of an adviser is to advise. The risk profiling process should lead to a conclusion as to what attitude to risk is most appropriate for your circumstances. A discussion should then take place to confirm this. In order to illustrate why this may be necessary, we will use an example of a cautious investor. Although they may be cautious by nature, they may be prepared to take a medium attitude to risk with regards to their retirement planning. This could be because they have been advised that their existing pension forecast is not projected to reach their income goal in retirement. Their choice would then be to either accept the shortfall or look towards taking a higher risk than they would usually be comfortable in taking. This is based on the belief - the higher the risk – the higher the return.

MAIN POINTS TO CONSIDER

✓ The main factors that have an impact on attitude to risk are – purpose, period and amount of the investment.

✓ The older you get, the more cautious you are likely to become.

✓ Lifestyling is a method where pensions (mainly) move to safer funds as you get closer to retirement.

✓ Risk profile questionnaires are used as a method of determining attitude to risk although they are not fool-proof.

✓ Investment risk cannot be eliminated although it can be minimised.

✓ There are different types of risk other than just the risk of losing your capital.

✓ If you are saving/investing for more than one purpose, your attitude to risk may differ as the purpose, timescales and amounts will also differ.

✓ Your attitude to risk will rarely remain constant and will vary depending on your circumstances.

FINAL THOUGHTS

■ Do I know what level of risk I am prepared to accept?

■ Do I know whether my current investments/funds reflect my attitude to risk?

■ Am I aware of all the risks associated with investing other than just the risk of losing my investment?

■ Is my attitude to risk ever re-appraised?

■ Is my retirement fund arranged so that it is switched to more cautious investments as my retirement draws nearer?

If you are not sure about the answers to any of the above questions, you may need help or advice in investigating matters further.

CHAPTER 8

WILLS AND ESTATE PLANNING

You may not automatically think of approaching a financial adviser when you are considering making a Will. The first port of call is likely to be a solicitor or possibly a Will writer. Nevertheless, I have included Wills and estate planning in this book because I firmly believe that a Will should be included in everybody's financial planning arrangements.

You can make plans to save for your retirement, save for other long term plans as well as ensure your family is protected against unforeseen circumstances. Ensuring your loved ones are passed down all that you have worked hard for throughout your life should be just as important.

Current statistics show that only 30% of people make a Will. Of those, many fail to keep their Will up to date. Whilst it is a fact that most people do not make a Will, there are many reasons why you should.

WHY MAKE A WILL?

1. To make sure your wishes are carried out.
2. For making gifts to specific people or charities.
3. To provide legacies, gifts, trusts.
4. To appoint Executors and Trustees.
5. To provide guardianship of minor children.
6. To reduce or eliminate Inheritance Tax duties.
7. To avoid dying intestate.

A well prepared Will gives you absolute peace of mind.

WHAT COULD HAPPEN IF I DON'T MAKE A WILL?

- You cannot be sure those you would want to benefit will actually do so.
- Your spouse may not automatically inherit your Estate.
- Minor children could be taken into care whilst guardians are appointed.
- There could be lengthy but yet avoidable delays for your beneficiaries.
- 'Common Law' partners may not receive anything.
- Disputes could easily arise if there is any uncertainty as to what is intended.

- If you leave your Estate to your children, they would receive any assets at age 18 whereas you may wish this to be delayed until age 21 or 25.

- More tax could be paid than would otherwise be necessary.

Sorting out who receives what can be expensive and the legal costs would be paid from your Estate.

WHAT ARE THE RULES OF INTESTACY?

The Rules of Intestacy date back to 1925. There are guidelines set down as to what happens to an Estate in the event of death. Needless to say, what you want to happen may not happen unless you make a Will.

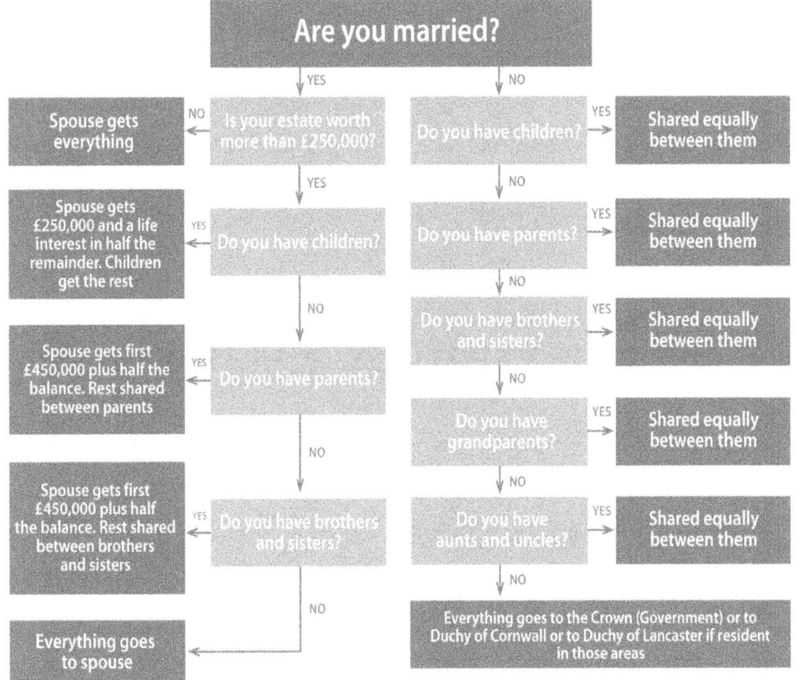

These rules change slightly where a spouse is non-UK domiciled. If you were therefore not born in the UK, you may wish to look into this further and this may mean that there is even more reason why you should consider making a Will.

SHOULD I JUST DO MY OWN DIY WILL?

This is certainly the cheapest way of writing a Will. It is also better than not making a Will at all. At least, all those remaining will have some idea of your wishes and intentions.

The basic problem with DIY Wills is at they tend to be ambiguous. If, for instance, you wanted to leave all your worldly goods to 'your children', you may not include any children that are yet to be born. If one of your children pre-deceases you, would you want their share to be re-distributed amongst your other children or passed down to the deceased's children?

If there was any uncertainty at all regarding some of the phrases used, whether and how it was witnessed, whether you were of sound mind or what your precise intentions were .... there could easily be problems.

SHOULD I USE ONE OF THE 'FREE' WILL WRITING SERVICES AVAILABLE?

The saying goes, "there is no such thing as a free lunch". This saying extends to Will writing as well.

If you use a bank to arrange your Will, they may want you to appoint them as Executor. By appointing your bank as Executor, they may charge up to 5% of the gross value of your Estate on death. For an Estate of £200,000, that is a cost of £10,000. Although the drafting of the Will may be free, there would be a significant cost based on that scenario. Charities also often prepare 'free' Wills. If your intention is to leave all, or a proportion, of your Estate to a charity then this option may be worth considering.

Most 'free' Wills I have seen tend to be very basic. They do not generally cater for all scenarios. If your affairs are not that straightforward, you may want to look towards other options.

SHOULD I USE A SOLICITOR OR A WILL WRITER?

There are arguments either way.

One Will writer put in his publicity that solicitors are "often not specifically trained in WILL writing as they cover many issues of law". I personally think this is a harsh generalisation. My experience is that the larger solicitor practices will have solicitors specifically designated to deal with Wills and trusts and will not be generalists as per this accusation.

The problem is that Will writing is not a regulated activity. Anyone can become a Will writer. Nevertheless, there has been a degree of professionalism introduced to this area of activity.

There is a professional body called 'The Society of Will Writers' and many Will writers choose to join in a bid to demonstrate their professionalism. They have a code of practice for their members to abide by and also stipulate that their members have the appropriate Professional Indemnity (PI) insurance.

Another reputable organisation, the Society of Trust and Estate Practitioners (STEPS), also sets high standards. They also have a code of professional conduct. As the title of the organisation suggests, their aims encompass trust and Estate planning rather than just Wills.

A solicitor may maintain that there isn't any degree of guaranteed professionalism in dealing with a Will writer, unlike solicitors that are governed by the Law Society.

The truth is that there are good Wills that are prepared by solicitors and Will writers alike. Equally, there are Wills prepared by some Will writers and some solicitors that are less than adequate.

ARE THERE ANY CIRCUMSTANCES WHERE MY WILL WOULD NEED TO BE UPDATED?

A Will can be invalidated by certain events such as marriage. In addition, your wishes may change over time and you may therefore wish to review your Will periodically.

A previous Will may be invalidated or, at least, should be re-written because of any of the following events:

■ *Marriage or re-marriage* – all Wills made before the date of the marriage are invalidated unless it is expressly stated in the Will that the intended marriage shall not revoke it.

■ *Divorce* – although divorce does not invalidate a Will, any appointment of the former spouse as an Executor or Trustee is treated as omitted, after the decree absolute.

■ *Separation* – this has no effect on the spouse's rights no matter how long the separation has lasted.

■ *Co-habitation* - a common law partner is not normally entitled to anything unless they are specifically mentioned in the Will or they can show dependency.

■ *Births or deaths* – the birth of children or death of a beneficiary may lead to a re-think as to how the Estate should be re-distributed. The death of a potential guardian may also require another to be appointed.

- *Changes in assets* – a significant change of assets may require documenting and consideration given to their eventual disposal.

- *Business changes* – whether you start your own business or become a shareholder, director or partner in a firm will probably result in a re-assessment of how these assets should be dealt with. For instance, you may want your share in any business to be passed to a family member who is likely to continue in the business and this would need to be specifically dealt with.

WHERE SHOULD I STORE MY WILL?

Let us imagine a scenario: After having the intention for many months/years, you finally get around to making a Will. It is likely to have taken you both money and a great deal of time and deliberation in getting this completed. After you have eventually passed away, no one can find the Will. In this scenario you may as well not have written one because, if the Will can't be found, you will have effectively died intestate.

Let's take another scenario: You have placed the Will with all your other valued documents at home. It is probably in a safe place where your relatives can find it. You have taken the decision to leave one of your closest relatives out of the Will but yet they are the ones to find it first. If they don't agree with your decision to leave them out of the Will, they may decide to destroy the evidence. Again, you may as well not have bothered.

The independent storage of your Will is very important in order to ensure your wishes are not only taken forward but are carried out in full. Many solicitors will provide this facility as part of their service. Will writers usually offer storage facilities for a fee.

Wherever your Will is kept, tell your executor(s) where it is. Keep it with your other important papers so that everything is together in one (hopefully secure) place.

In order to make doubly safe, you may choose to register the fact there is a Will. This would also provide the Executors and your close relatives with the details of the whereabouts of the Will. In the United Kingdom, there is no central register of Wills. There are one or two private companies that offer a registration service for a fee. As part of the registration process, you can say where your Will is kept. By registering your Will in this way, this should give extra security and peace of mind that your wishes will be carried out as per your last Will and testament. As mentioned, there is no compulsion to register Wills and registering your Will in this way is, by no means, foolproof.

WHAT IS ESTATE PLANNING?

This is the process of anticipating and preparing for the disposal of an Estate. Estate planning typically attempts to eliminate uncertainties over the administration of probate and maximise the value of the estate by reducing taxes and other expenses.

In practice, it is the use of Wills and trusts designed to protect and preserve your wealth for the next or even subsequent generations. It may be that you are looking to avoid or reduce any liability to Inheritance Tax (IHT). The avoidance of paying long term care costs could be another objective. A further consideration could be in respect of leaving your wealth to your children whilst looking to ensure that any existing or future in-laws would not benefit if they later became divorced.

Whilst the purpose of this book is to help you decide whether you need advice in certain areas, estate planning is an area where costly mistakes can be made by trying to do it yourself. In my opinion, advice should be obtained in the vast majority of instances.

CAN I AVOID PAYING INHERITANCE TAX (IHT)?

A properly drafted Will can be the cornerstone of minimising any death duties/ Inheritance Tax (IHT).

Lord Jenkins, when he was the Chancellor of the Exchequer, famously referred to Inheritance Tax as "a voluntary levy paid by those who distrust their heirs more than they dislike the Inland Revenue". Whether this statement is true or not, there is much that you can do to minimise any IHT duties.

You can eliminate IHT altogether by giving all or nearly all your assets away. This is a bit extreme. Nevertheless, any improvement on taking no action at all can improve matters. Some options that are available can be broadly summarised as the following:

1. Spend before you die.
2. Give away assets to individuals, charities or to a trust.
3. Write a tax efficient Will.
4. Create a fund that you have access to but yet falls
   outside your Estate.
5. Create a fund, or take out life cover, to pay your IHT bill.

Any action that is taken will probably need to be reviewed each year as your circumstances, and even the Inheritance Tax threshold (referred to as the Nil rate band), are likely to change.

WHAT CAN I DO TO AVOID LONG TERM CARE COSTS?

It could be argued that you should do nothing. After all, isn't it fair that we should all do our bit to pay for the costs associated with the care of the elderly?

That is one view. Another view that is often put forward is along the lines of – 'I have worked hard all my life to gather all the possessions I have. I want to do all that I can to protect these for my family rather than for these to be taken by the authorities'.

An estimated 70,000 people per year have to sell their homes to pay for care.

There are steps that can be taken to ensure your Estate is protected. Extreme care must be taken so that you are fully aware of any repercussions. I would recommend that advice is sought in this area as serious mistakes can be, and have been, made.

One of the main doctrines that applies when looking at passing assets on to others comes under the heading of 'deliberate deprivation of assets'. If the Local Authority believes that funds are being given away as a method of avoiding care costs, they will challenge this. If they believe that the Estate has been deliberately reduced in order to influence the care assessment, they would treat such a gift as though it never happened.

Also, be wary of the pre-owned assets tax (POAT). This is a tax that applies where an owner of a property gives it away but yet continues to live in it.

IS THERE ANYTHING THAT I CAN DO TO PREVENT THE IN-LAWS GETTING ACCESS TO AN INHERITANCE?

The answer is YES. It would involve trusts whether they were established by trust deed or as part of Will planning.

The idea basically involves leaving any assets to a trust rather than to an individual. If, say, you wanted to leave your Estate to your daughter but was concerned about who she was married to, you may want to leave your Estate to a trust instead. A typical arrangement would involve leaving your Estate to a trust instead of your daughter. In the example I have just given, the daughter would be able to borrow funds from the trust. If she later became divorced, there would be no claims on those funds as they would need to be paid back to the trust. Although she would enjoy the assets, there would be a corresponding debt created to prevent there being a claim in divorce or even bankruptcy.

MAIN POINTS TO CONSIDER

✓ The only way to ensure your Estate is dealt with in the way you wish is to make a Will.

✓ Your Will should be kept in a secure place.

✓ Try to ensure all those who need to know are able to locate your Will when it is needed.

✓ Estate planning is way of preserving your wealth for future generations.

✓ Estate planning often needs to take into account a number of different situations.

✓ With Estate planning, seeking advice is strongly recommended.

✓ Inheritance Tax can be minimised or even avoided with careful planning.

FINAL THOUGHTS

- Does my Will reflect my current wishes?

- Does my Will need updating or amending?

- What will happen to my Estate when I die? Where do the assets go?

- Does my family know where to find my Will?

- Do my family know about all my savings, investments, life cover and pension arrangements?

- Do I know how much would be payable in Inheritance Tax when I die?

- Am I concerned about my children inheriting money at age 18? Would they be able to spend the money wisely?

- Am I worried about my children inheriting my Estate and then half these funds being paid out in a divorce settlement?

If you are not sure about the answers to any of the above questions, you may need help or advice in investigating matters further.

CONCLUSION

Now you have almost reached the end of this book, I hope that you have found the previous pages informative and that it has made you think about your financial plans.

There are a number of objectives that I hope have been met.

The first of these was in respect of Chapter One – "Your objectives and needs". The question is for those who haven't written any financial goals – "Will you do so now?" If you feel that you need help with putting together (and reviewing) your financial plan, that is a very good reason why you need help and assistance. A competent financial planner (not a salesman) will help you achieve this.

If, on the other hand, you feel as though you can do this yourself, then there will be no need for you to pay for professional help in this respect. All you will need is self-discipline, commitment and prioritisation. You may also need to accumulate extra skills and knowledge if you want to be a 'do-it-yourselfer'.

The majority of people unfortunately do not make any goals whether they be financial goals or otherwise. They just take each day as it comes. For those of you who fall into that category, Chapter One may not have been that relevant. Nevertheless, it must be stressed that those who do start a pension do so because they have a goal to have more money in retirement. If not, why start a pension in the first place? You may as well just spend the money.

A danger that affects us all is associated with our current pace of life. We are all so much more 'connected' than we used to be. There are so many more demands on our time. Time gets taken up with the urgent things whether they are important or not so important. I would consider planning for your retirement as being important. When you are young, retirement planning is not so urgent. As you get older, this changes. If this is a danger for you, you may choose to use the services of an adviser just to help establish some self-discipline in making sure you have a plan and that it remains on track.

The need to review your plans on a frequent basis was also emphasised. Throughout the book, I have pressed the need to review your arrangements on a regular basis. Too many times, I have seen situations where a plan has been put in place and not reviewed. Sometimes, clients cannot even remember why they started a particular policy in the first place. Plans can quickly become outdated due to any number of reasons. These can include a change in circumstances as well as inflationary pressures effectively devaluing whatever you have in place.

Another objective that I hope has been achieved is to highlight the difference as to when you can do-it-yourself and when it would be foolish to even contemplate that.

In Chapter 8, I emphasised the need for advice to be sought when looking at Estate planning. You could possibly avoid the need for advice if you were to buy an 'off the shelf' Will and write it yourself. You could also possibly calculate the amount of Inheritance tax you were liable for. Where advice would most definitely be needed is in connection with the legal consequences of Estate planning and any attempt to avoid long term care costs.

Another factor to consider is associated with the ever changing face of financial services and with newer innovative products being introduced. Take retirement planning, for instance. I could highlight temporary, fixed term or variable annuities as being prime examples. These are just some of the innovations seen in the 'at retirement' market. How can you possibly begin to arrange your own income in retirement if you don't even know such plans exist let alone know how these could easily be the best option available to you?

On the other side of the coin, financial advice can be costly. Are you getting value for money? Could you obtain the information/advice elsewhere for a lower charge?

Some advisers charge for the initial advice, setting up the plans as well as an ongoing charge. This ongoing charge can be by way of, say, a monthly retainer or by way of a percentage charge for funds under management. It may be transparent what costs are incurred. With other arrangements, it may not be clear to you. Do you know how much you are paying your adviser? Half a per cent or 1% per annum may not sound much but this could equate to a significant sum of money if you calculate this in money terms.

The quality of the advisers is undoubtedly improving. Equally, the number of advisers is falling. You may find it harder now to obtain financial advice compared with even just a few years ago. Many of us can remember representatives from Pearl, Refuge, Co-Op (and many other insurance companies) calling at their home collecting premiums and providing a service for all the family. Those days are very much a thing of the past. There was also a time when the banks lost very little opportunity in mentioning their financial advice service at virtually every opportunity. More recently, some banks have taken the decision to significantly reduce the number of advisers they employ.

To compensate for there being fewer advisers, there is much more information available than there used to be.

There are a host of websites out there offering free information. Some of these are paid for from the advertising revenue they earn. Some websites claim to be informative but may have an underlying sales objective. I will give special mention to two public websites that have no hidden agenda other than to provide to the public free advice.

1. The Money Advice Service (www.moneyadviceservice.org.uk) offers free guidance and information booklets designed to help and assist with many different financial situations. This can range from retirement planning, savings and investments and mortgages. You can even use this website to undergo a free financial health check which I would urge you to do.

2. The Pensions Advice Service (TPAS) is another free service. They can be contacted to obtain information regarding company and private pensions. They can also assist when there is a dispute. I have found their service to be extremely useful. (www.thepensionadvisoryservice.org.uk)

Ultimately, it is your decision whether to use the free information available and 'go it alone' or to utilise the services of an adviser to help you achieve your financial goals. Hopefully, this book has made you think again or, at least, provide you with more information from which to make an informed decision.